Francis Creek Fjords Coloring Books: Color Your Way Into Horseback Riding

ISBN-13: 978-0-9971624-4-8

Copyright © 2016 Francis Creek Fjords, LLC, Francis Creek, WI. All rights reserved.
Published by Francis Creek Fjords (www.FrancisCreekFjords.com). Printed by CreateSpace.

Patti Jo Walter and her husband, Dave Walter, started Francis Creek Fjords (FCF) in 1995. FCF was a Fjord hub for nearly two decades, having Fjords come from all over the United States to be trained, sold on consignment, or bred to their stallion, Fair Acres Ole. Patti Jo began giving riding lessons in 1998, teaching myriad disciplines: huntseat, dressage, jumping, and driving. Today, she continues to instruct dressage and jumping, sharing her passion with anyone wishing to learn and have fun with horses.

Inspired by Patti Jo Walt·

Patricia Holland, born and raised in Northeastern Pennsylvania, attended York Academy of Art to pursue a career in commercial art. Dovetailing her lifelong passions of art and horses, she became a professional horse trainer, illustrating what she saw, what she learned, and the people she met along the way. With humor and wit she juggles these contrasting careers, creating a rich and fulfilling life. She resides and illustrates in Galena, Illinois.

Illustrated by Pat Holland

Norwegian Fjord Horses (N.F.H.), featured in many of these drawings, are an offshoot horse breed well known for their gentle disposition, calm demeanor, and great versatility, but it's their loving and humorous personalities that draw in most owners. Mutual affection for these charismatic animals caused Pat and Patti's lives to intersect. Once united, Pat's humor and wit served as the perfect complement to Patti Jo's love of life, forging a lifelong friendship in and out of the pasture, much like the horses they admire.

Pat and Patti created this coloring book series as a fun way of learning horseback riding terminology and concepts for Francis Creek Fjords' students. Pat's skillfully drawn illustrations—filled with humor, life, and laughter—combined with Patti Jo's impressive understanding of horses and students resulted in a colorful array of barnyard characters teaching valuable horse-related lessons you can color.

How to use this book

Step 1: Grab your crayons or colored pencils! (Markers are not recommended)

....

Step 2: Choose your favorite picture!

....

Step 3: Color!

....

Step 4: Have fun!

....

Don't forget to read the notes and study the images. There are lessons to be learned within these pages.

So You Want to Ride a Horse?

Here's What You Need to Know

First there are two types of riding: English and Western

Western Rider

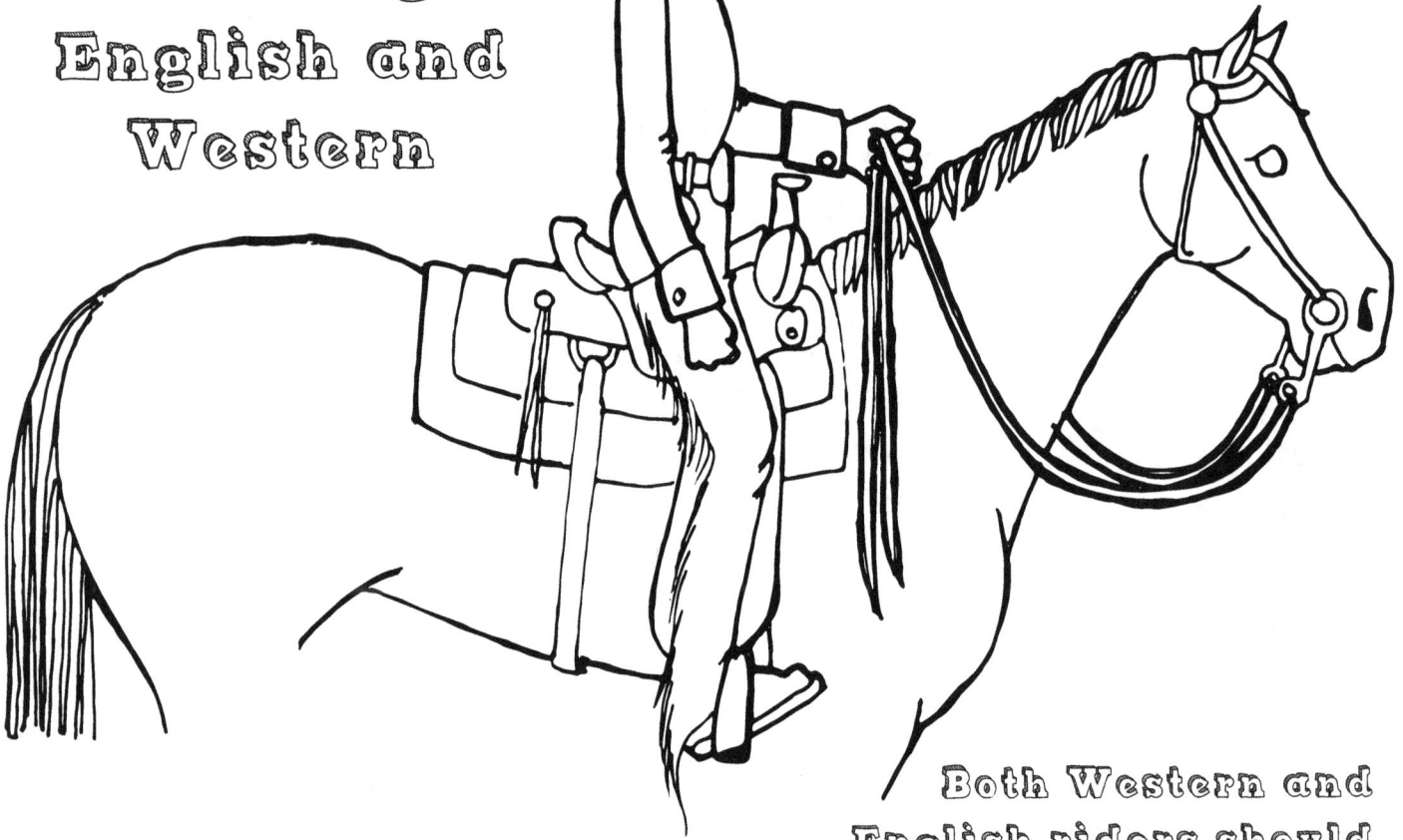

English Rider

Both Western and English riders should sit tall and straight in the saddle, with arms relaxed yet tight to their body, and legs hanging naturally along the horse's side.

Both have their own Tack (gear: saddles, bridles, etc.)

Horn

Cantle

Roll

Gullet

Saddle
Strings

Ladigo
Holder

Seat

Front
Rigging
Dee

Latigo

Flank
Billet

Skirt

Fender

Hobble
Strap

Flank
Cinch

Stirrup
Leather

Stirrup

Front
Cinch

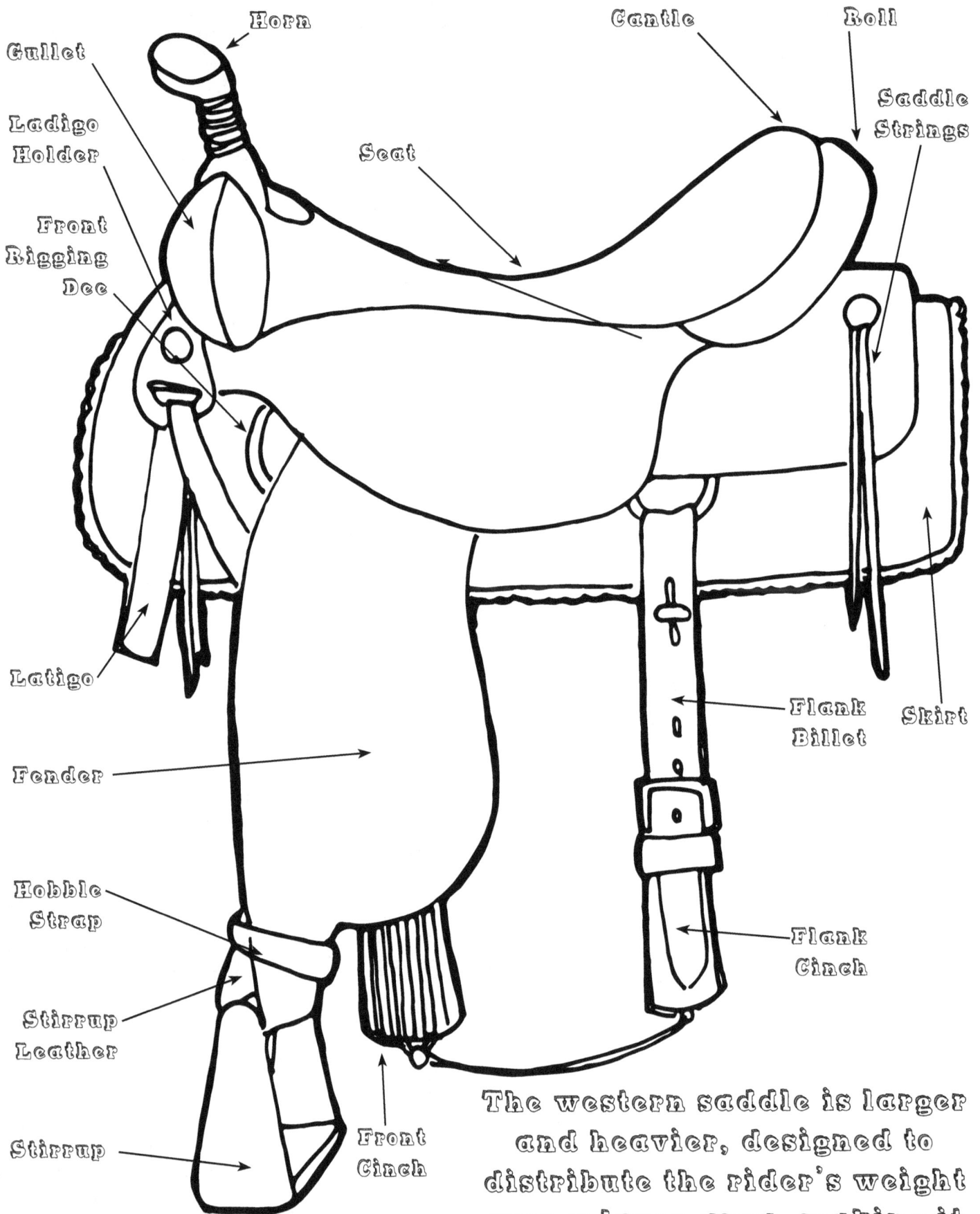

The western saddle is larger
and heavier, designed to
distribute the rider's weight
over a large area, making it
more comfortable.

Parts of a Western Saddle

Pommel

Seat

Knee
Roll

Cantle

Skirt

Panel

Flap

Leather

Girth

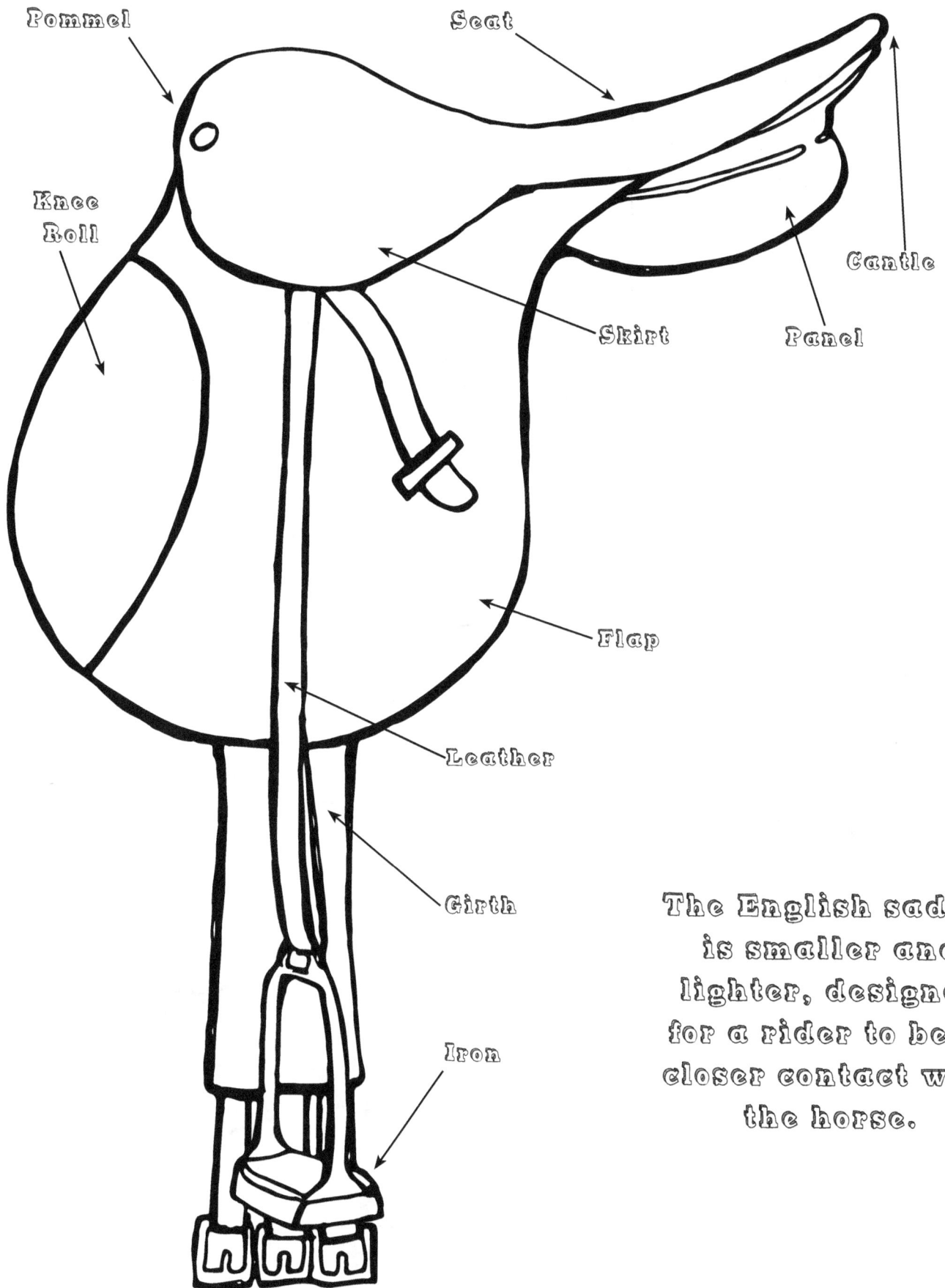

The English saddle
is smaller and
lighter, designed
for a rider to be in
closer contact with
the horse.

Iron

Parts of an English Saddle

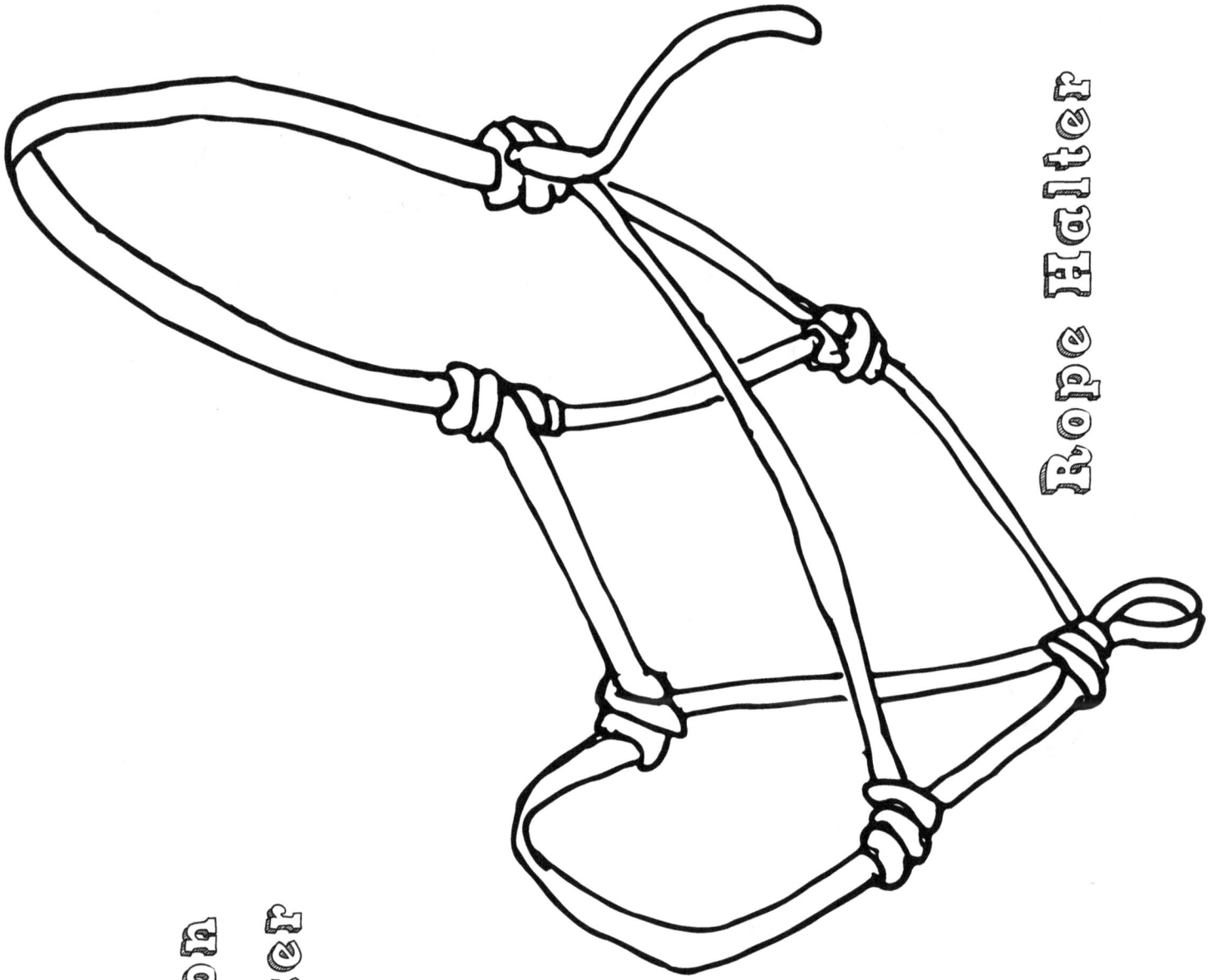

Rope Halter

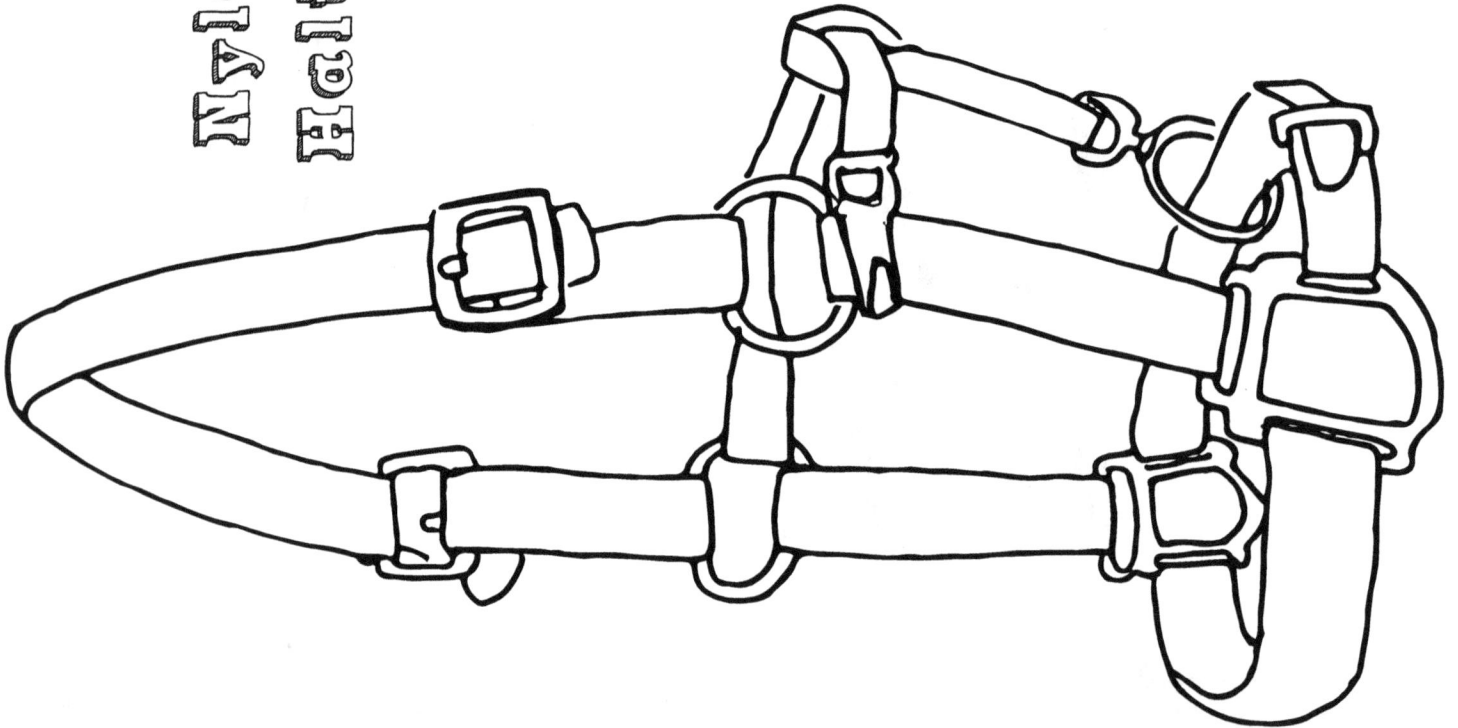

Nylon Halter

Browband

Crownpiece

Cheekpiece

Throatlatch

Noseband

Bit

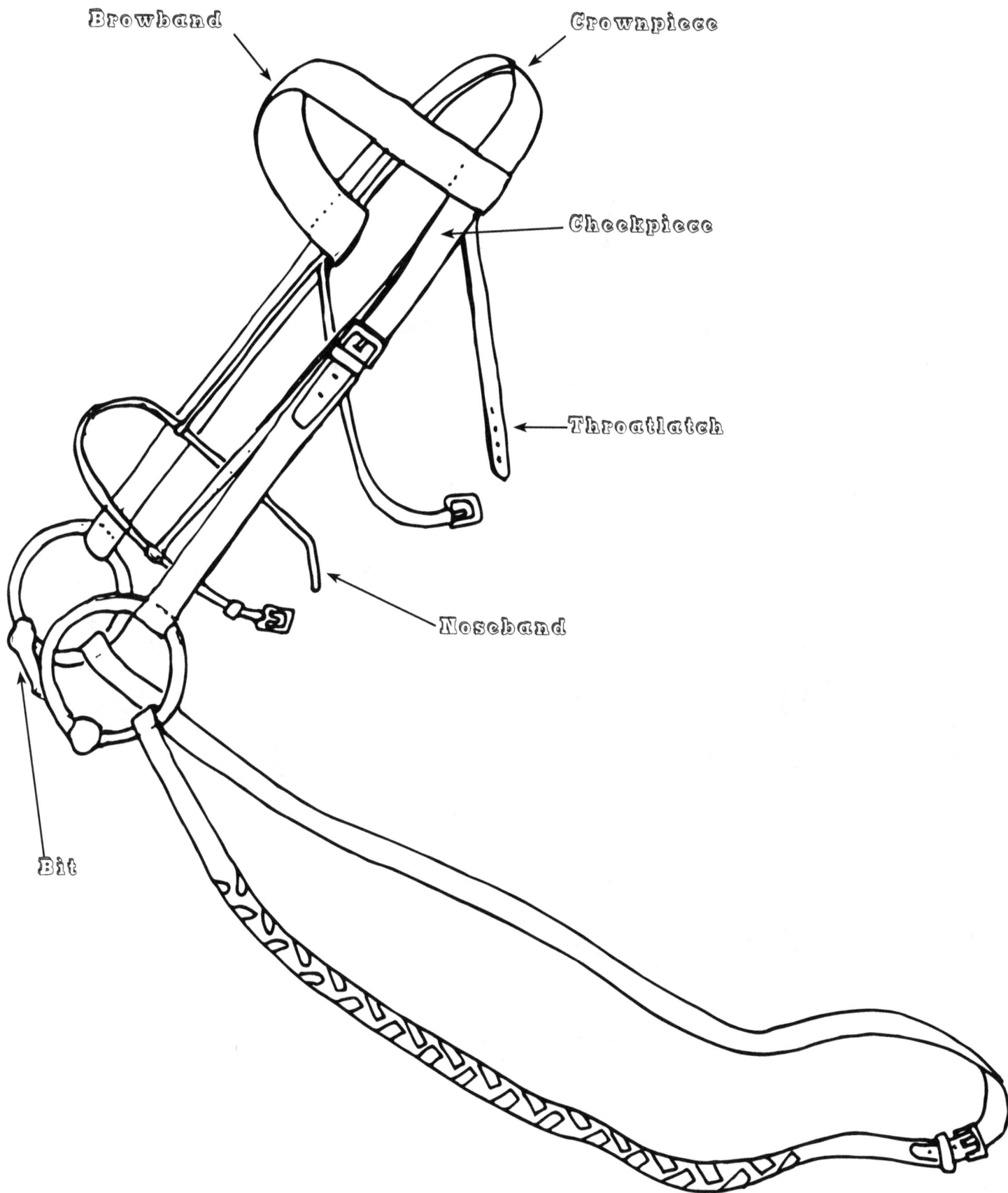

Parts of an English Bridle

Bitless Bridles

Mechanical Hackamore

Bitless bridles are often used to start young horses.

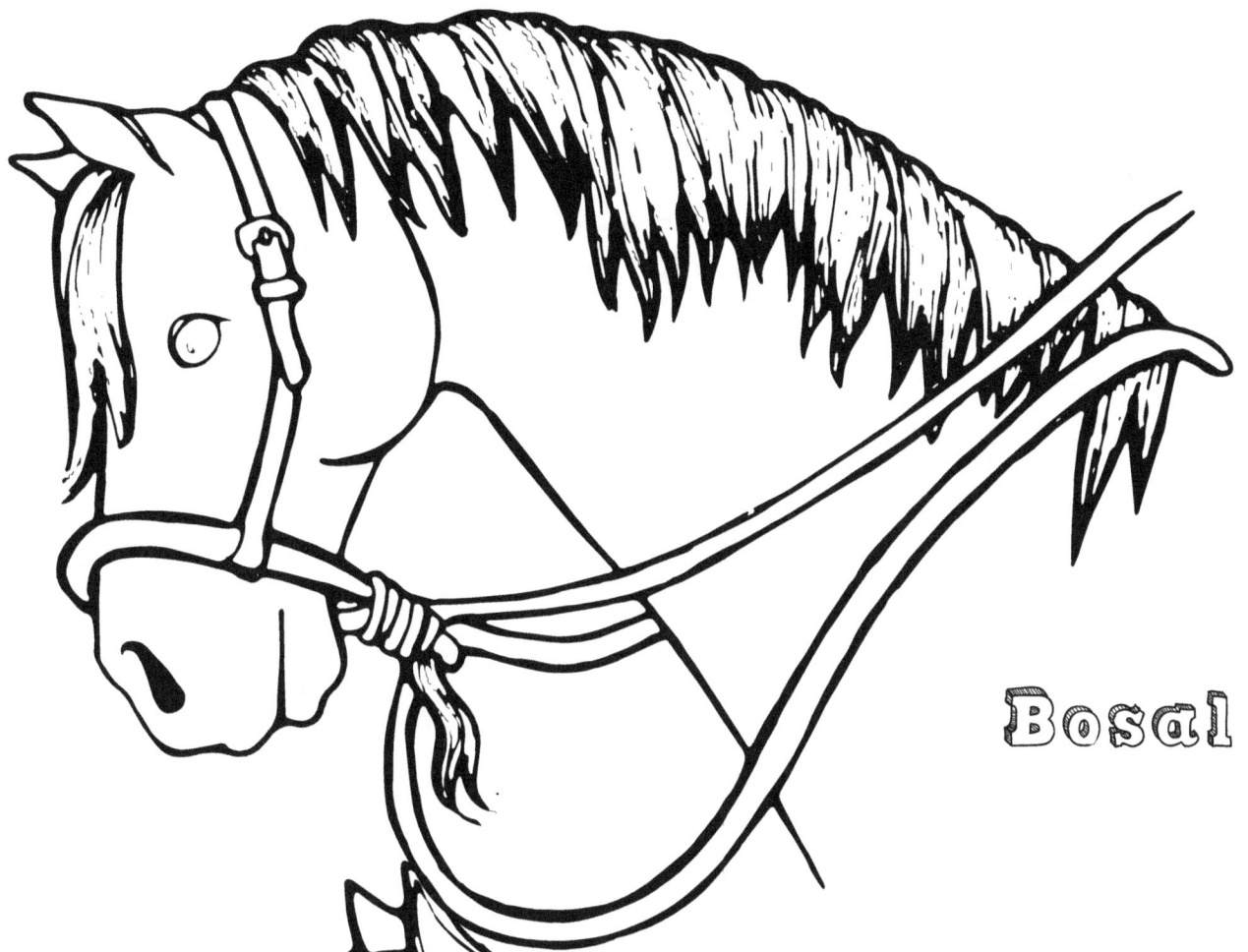

Bosal

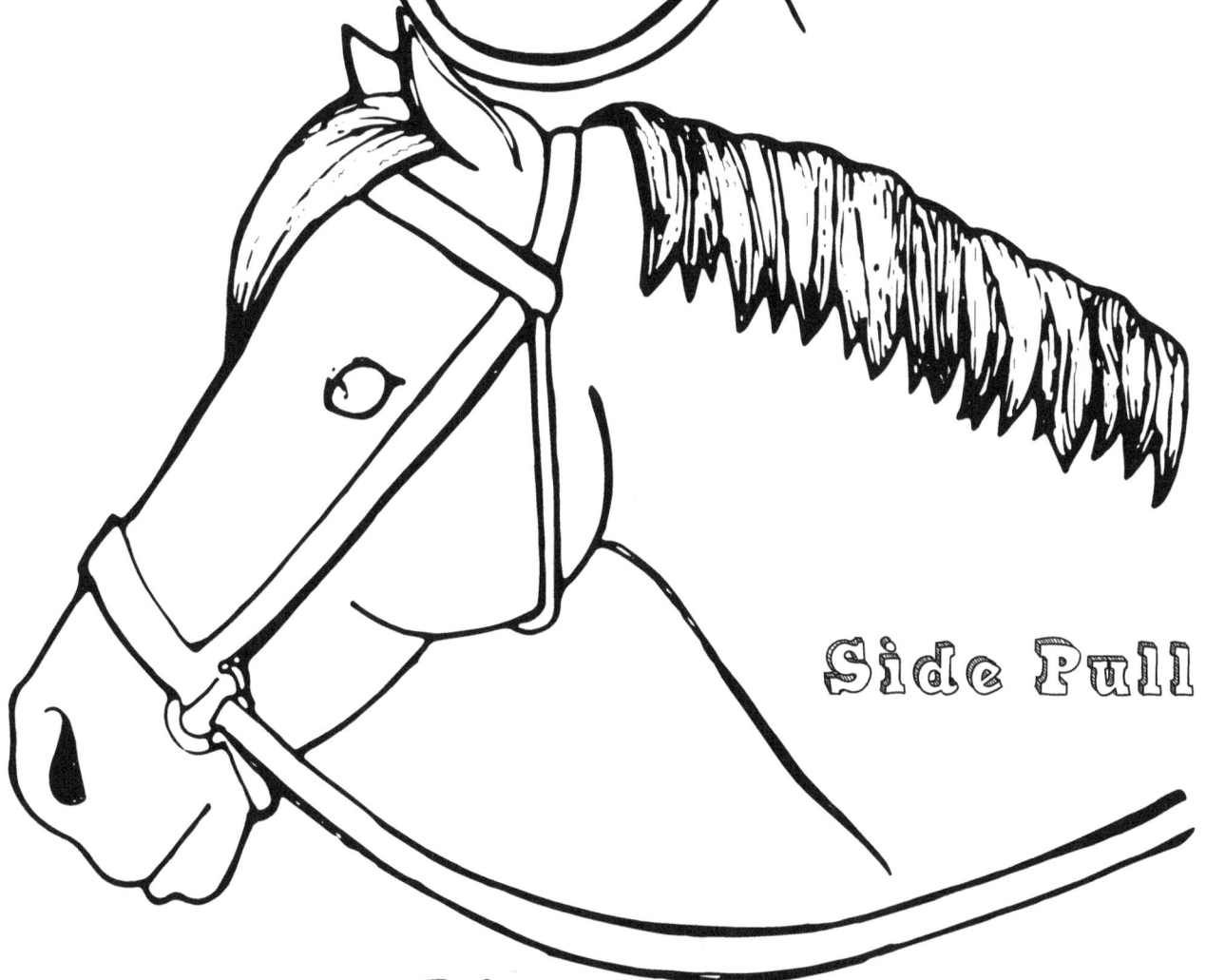

Side Pull

Western Bitless Bridles

Browband

Western Headstalls

One Ear

Vacquero
Crossover

Western Headstalls

Standing
Martingale

Martingales are
used to control
the horse's head
height

Running
Martingale

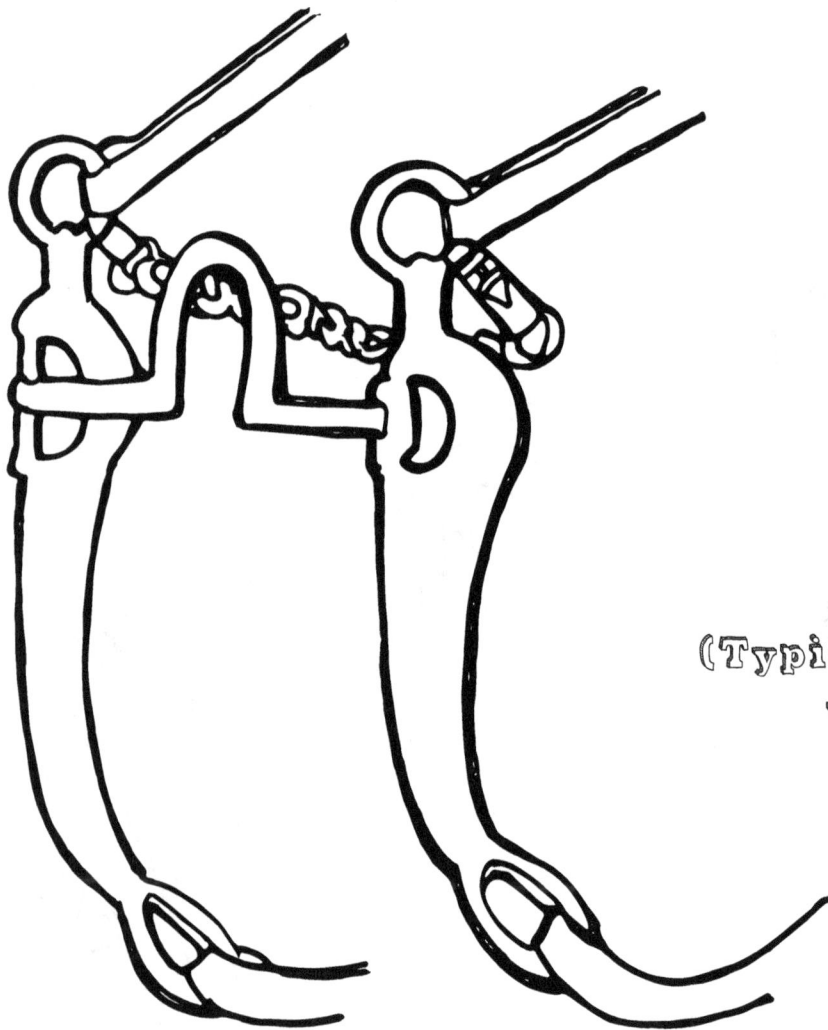

Curb
(Typical western bit
with port)

Snaffle
(Often used to start a
youngster)

(The more narrow the
mouth piece, the more
reactive it is.)

Types of Bits

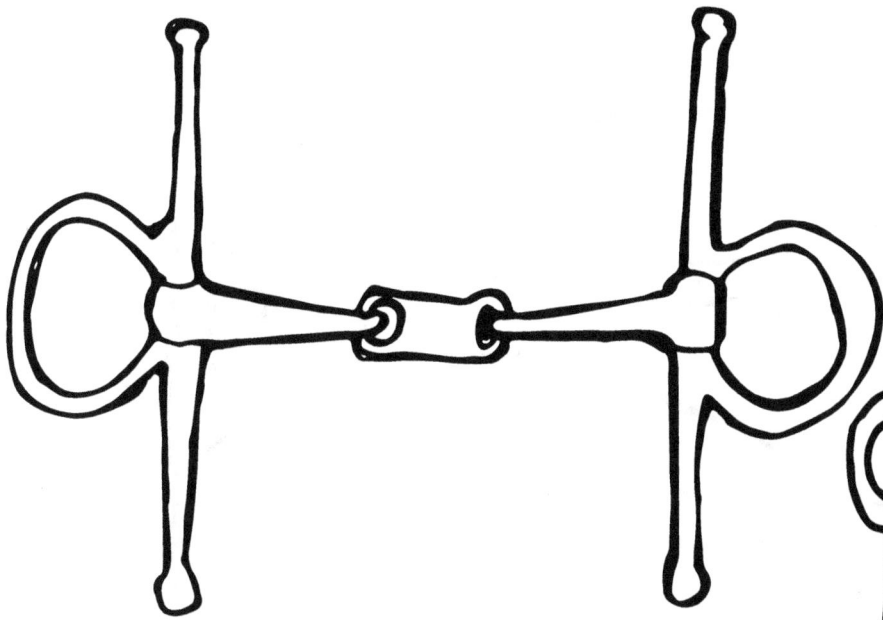

Dr. Bristol Full
Cheek Snaffle

Pelham
(elements of BOTH curb
and snaffle)

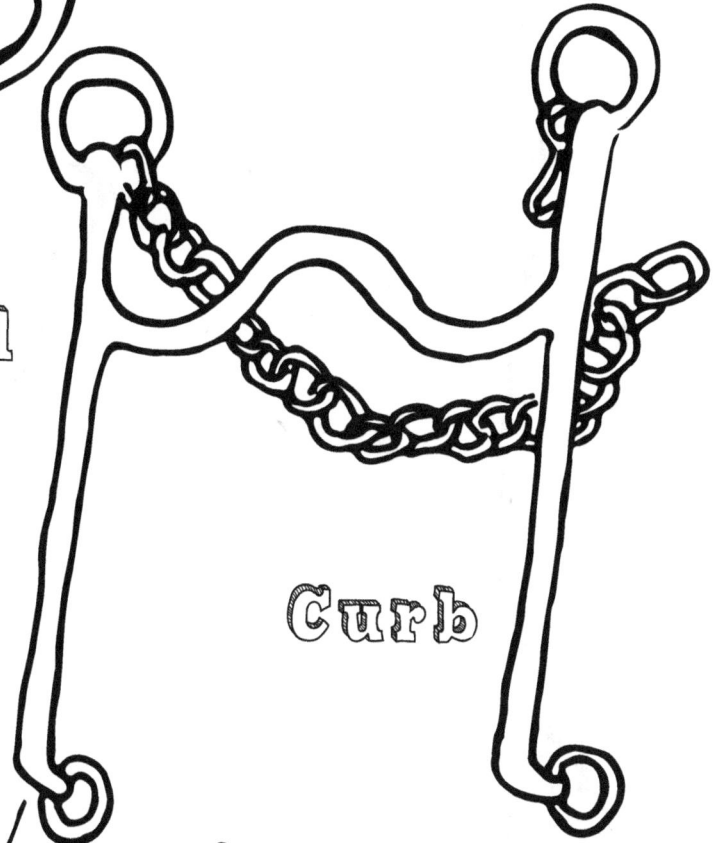

Curb

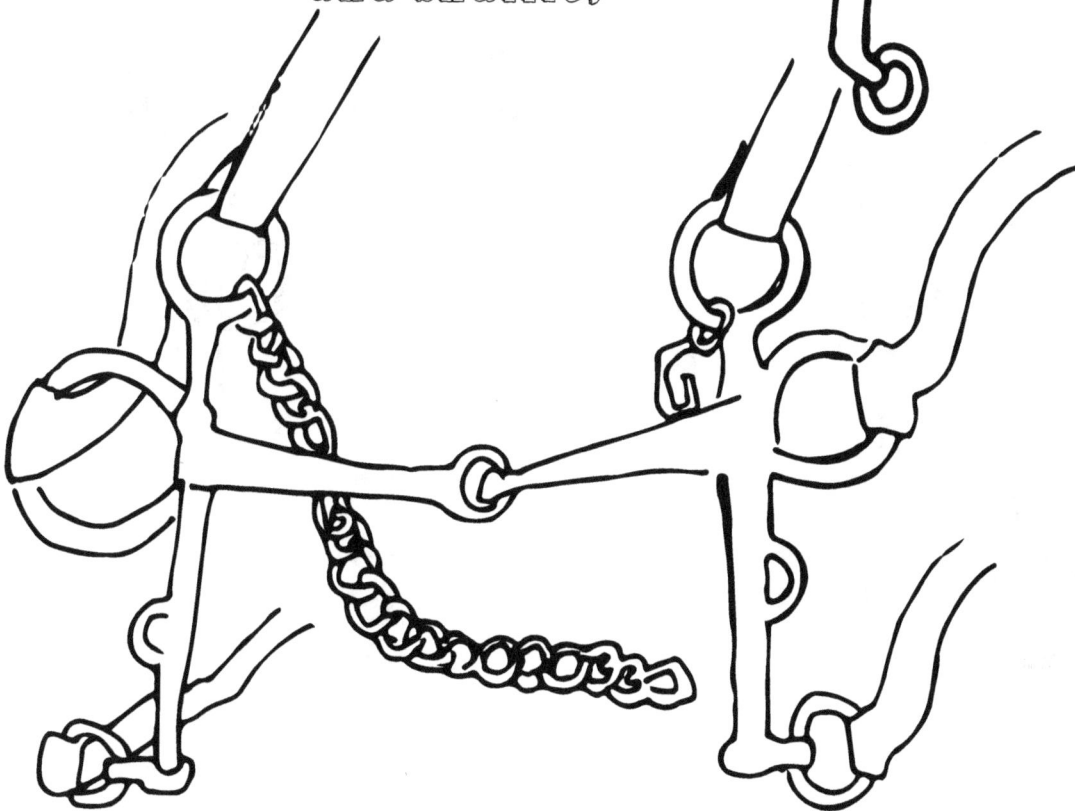

Types of English Bits

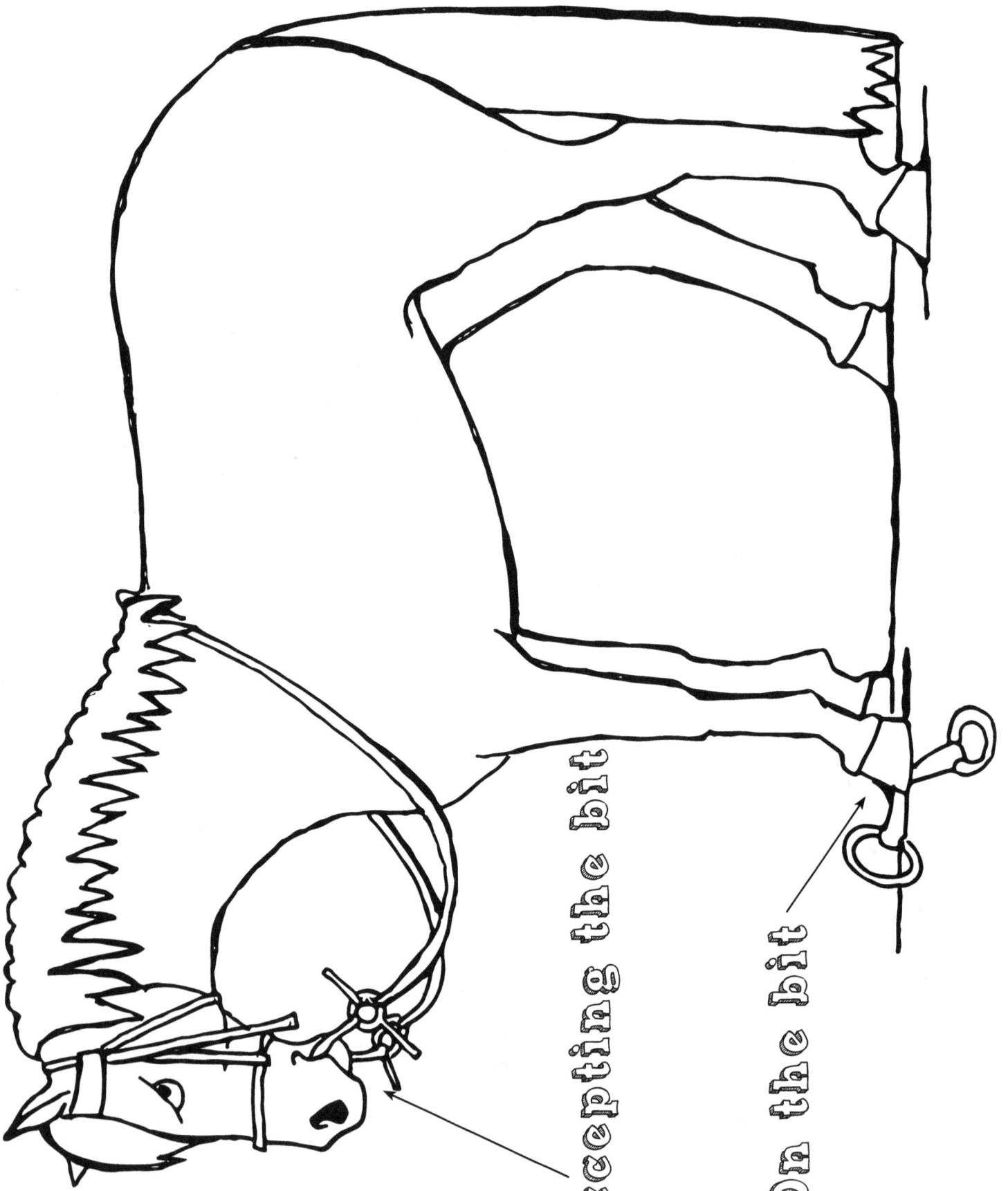

Accepting the bit

On the bit

Slobber Straps

Some Western riders use slobber straps, which were originally used close to the bit to avoid replacing the entire rein when it wears out. Today, slobber straps combined with heavy rope reins increase the amount of contact a rider has with the horse's mouth.

Romal Reins

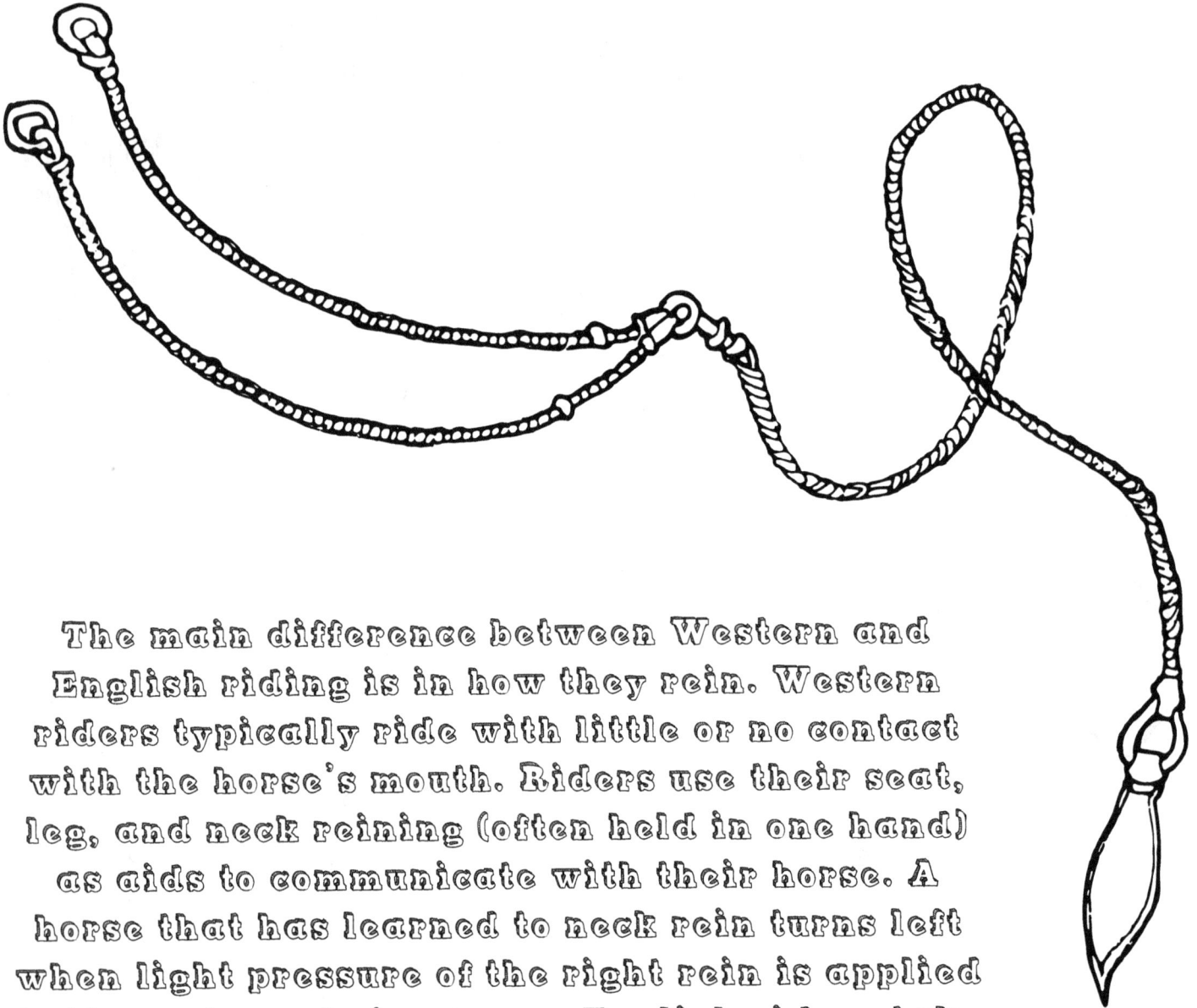

The main difference between Western and English riding is in how they rein. Western riders typically ride with little or no contact with the horse's mouth. Riders use their seat, leg, and neck reining (often held in one hand) as aids to communicate with their horse. A horse that has learned to neck rein turns left when light pressure of the right rein is applied to its neck, and vice versa. English riders take direct contact with the horse's mouth using the reins (held in both hands), seat, and leg as aids for speed and direction.

Romal reins, usually made of leather or rawhide, are connected to the bridle and used as a tool to assist in moving cattle.

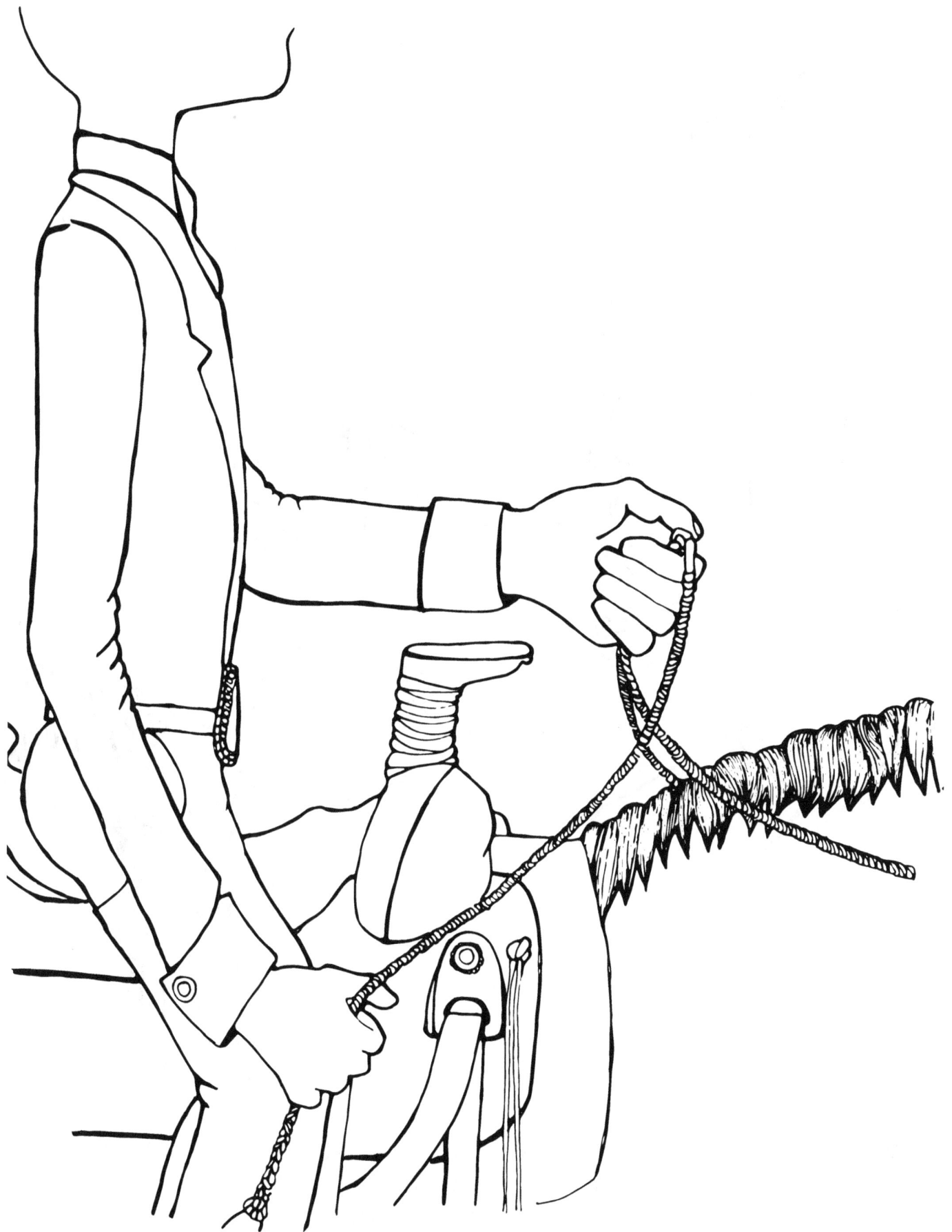

Proper Handset
with Romal Reins

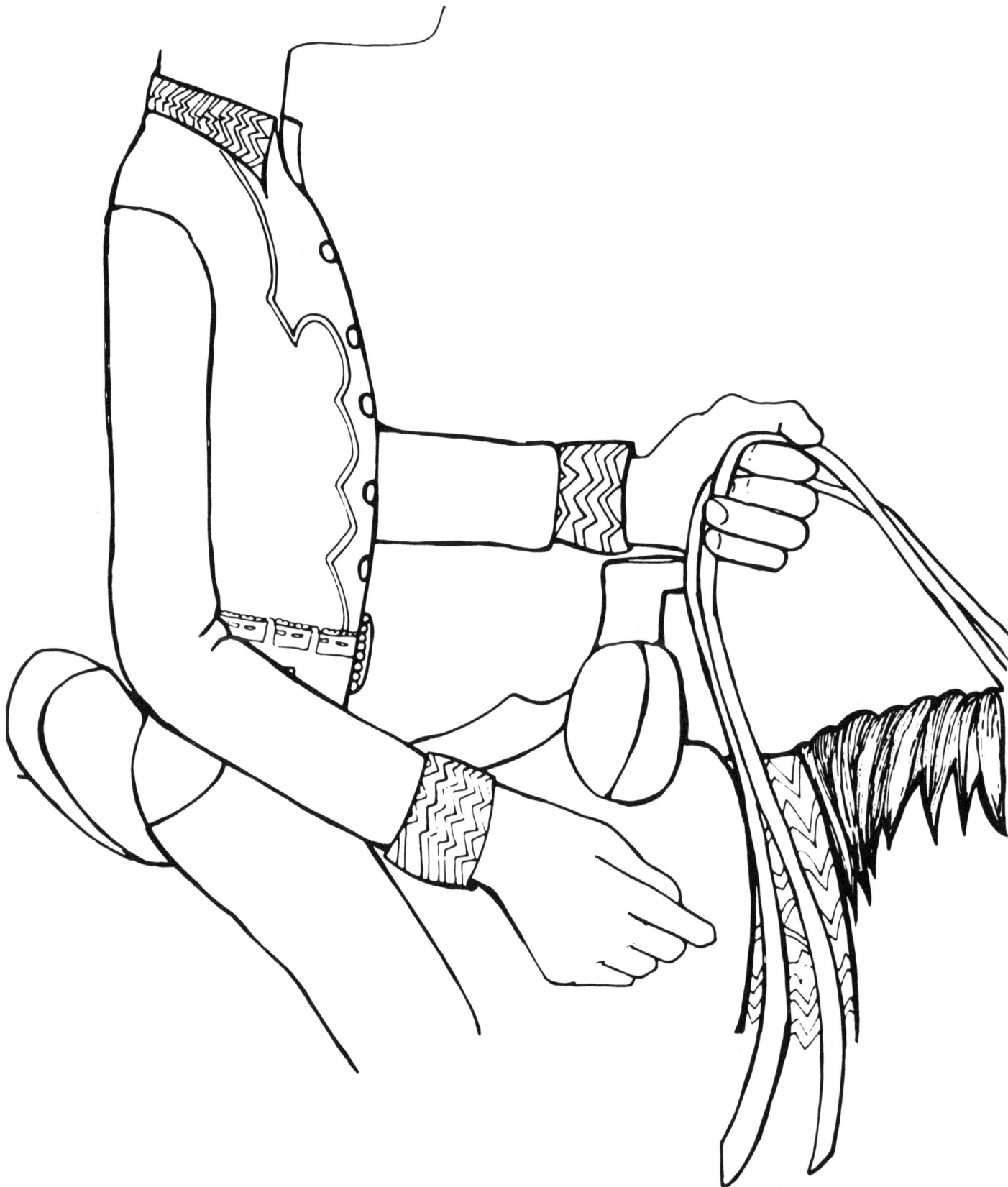

Western riders rode with one hand and neck reined because
they worked their ranches on horseback, using their other hand
to open and close gates and rope cattle.

Your index finger should be in between the reins, thumb on top,
with your other digits loosely supporting the reins.

How to Carry Split Reins

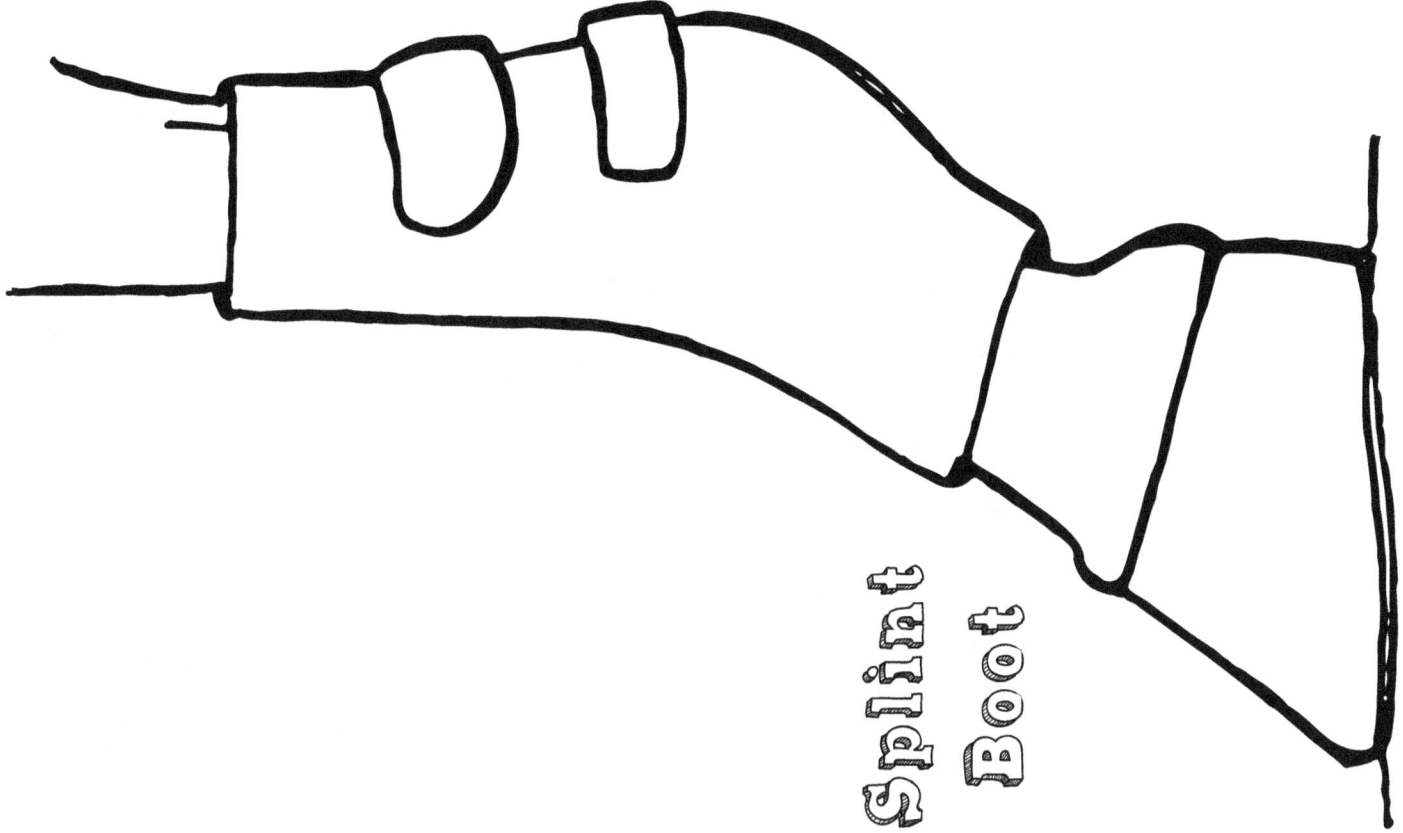

Splint
Boot

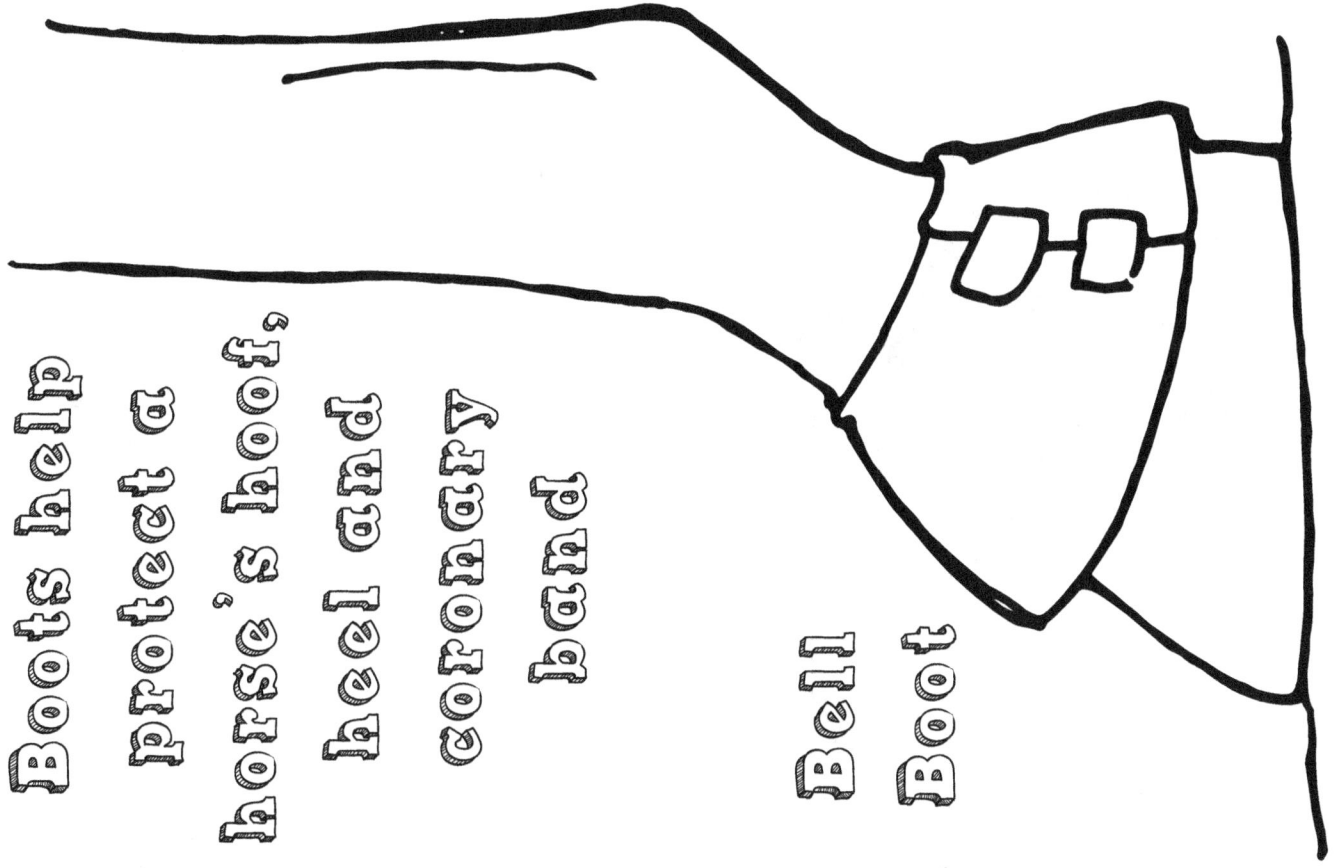

Boots help
protect a
horse's hoof,
heel and
coronary
band

Bell
Boot

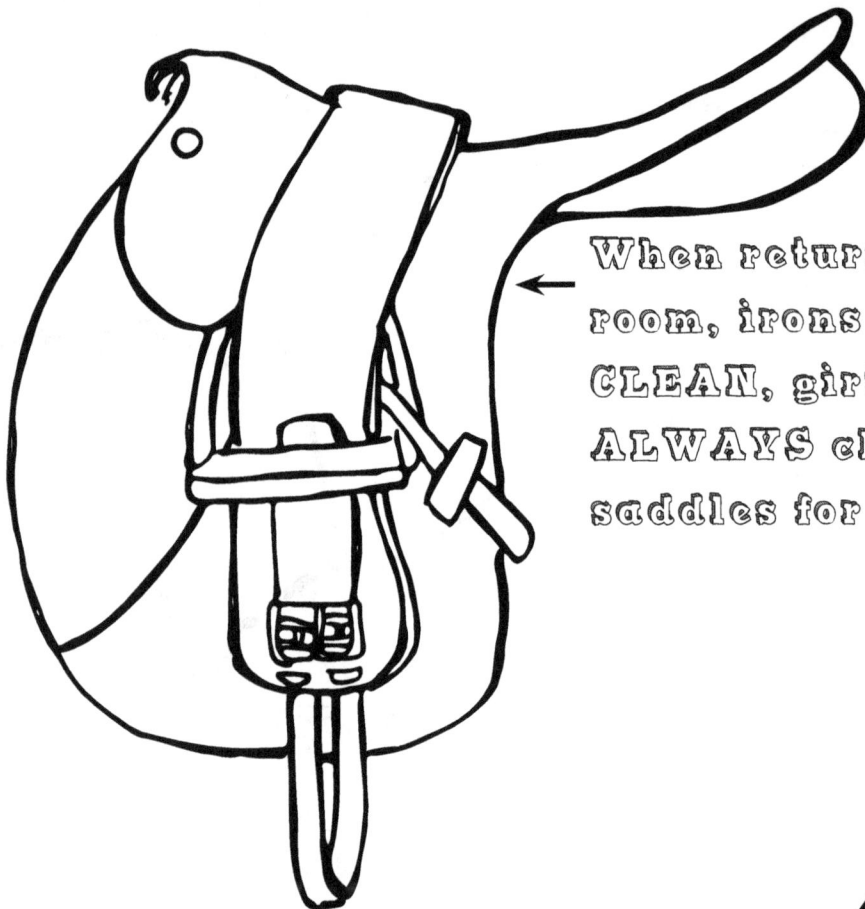

When returning saddle to tack room, irons should be run up and CLEAN, girth slotted from irons. ALWAYS clean and inspect saddles for wear.

A saddle returned to the tack room facing out, depicts a saddle that NEEDS cleaning.

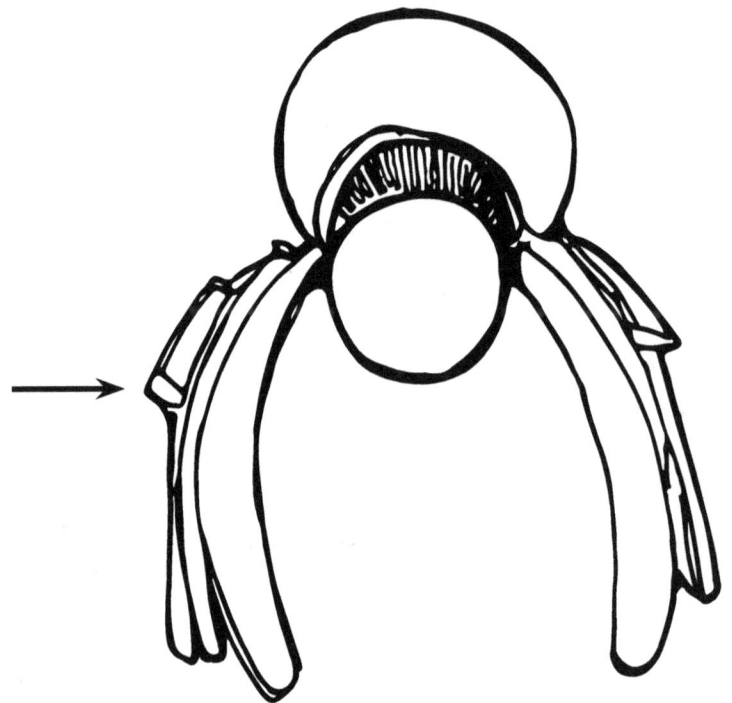

A saddle facing toward the wall NAMEPLATE SHOWN has been cleaned, inspected and ready for use.

Tack Room Etiquette

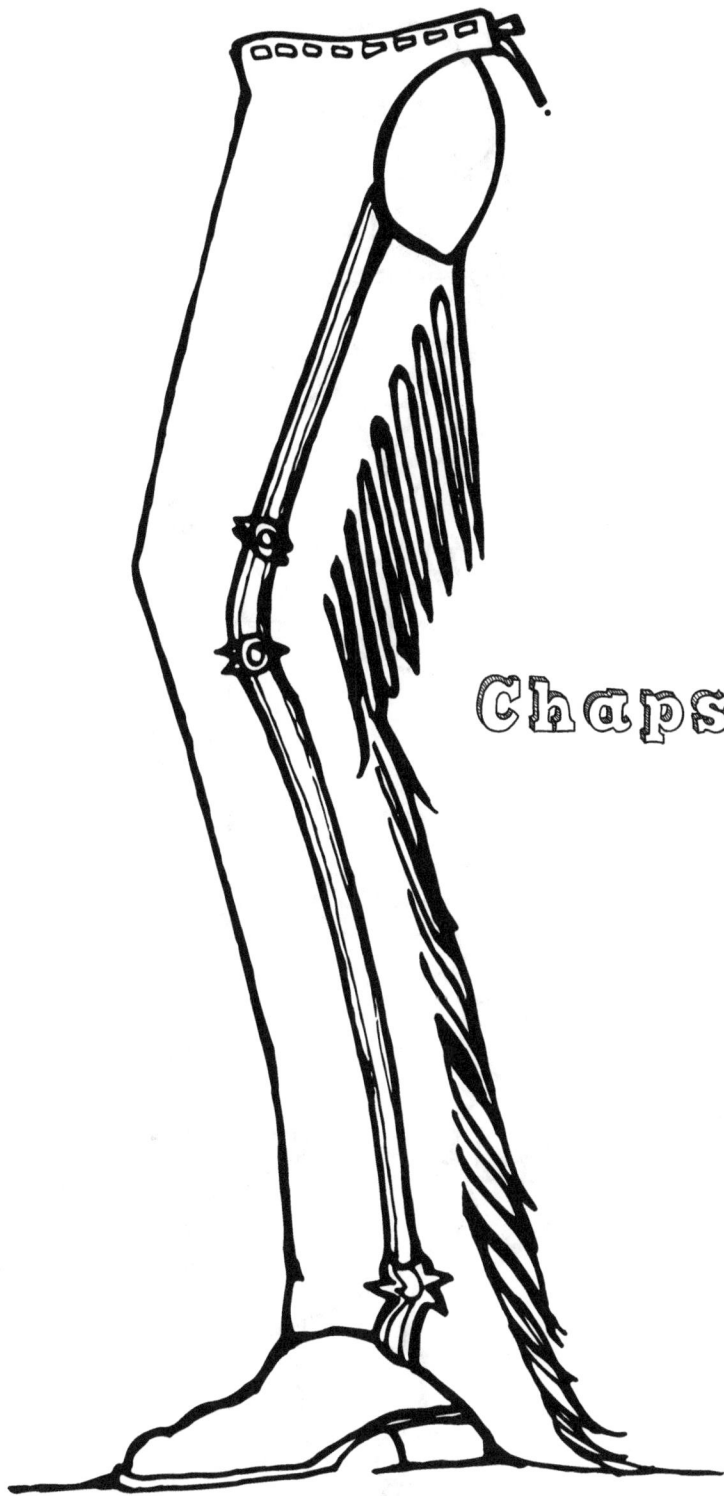

Chaps

Chinks

Western and English riders dress differently! You'll see pretty
standard Western attire throughout this book.

In hot climates, cowboys wear chinks, which are cooler and
allow for easier mounting and dismounting from their horse.

Chaps & Chinks

Hunt Seat Attire   Eventing Attire

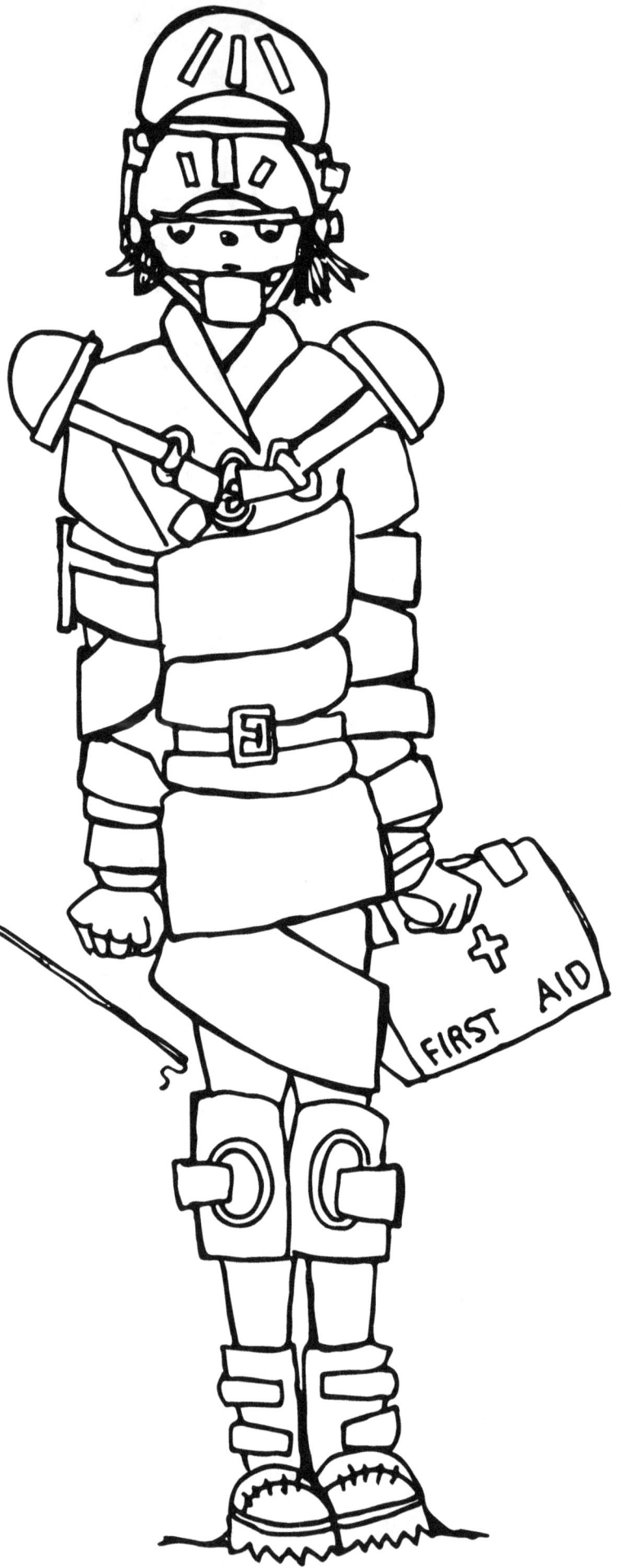

Ready to Ride? Not Yet! First You Must Know Yourself.

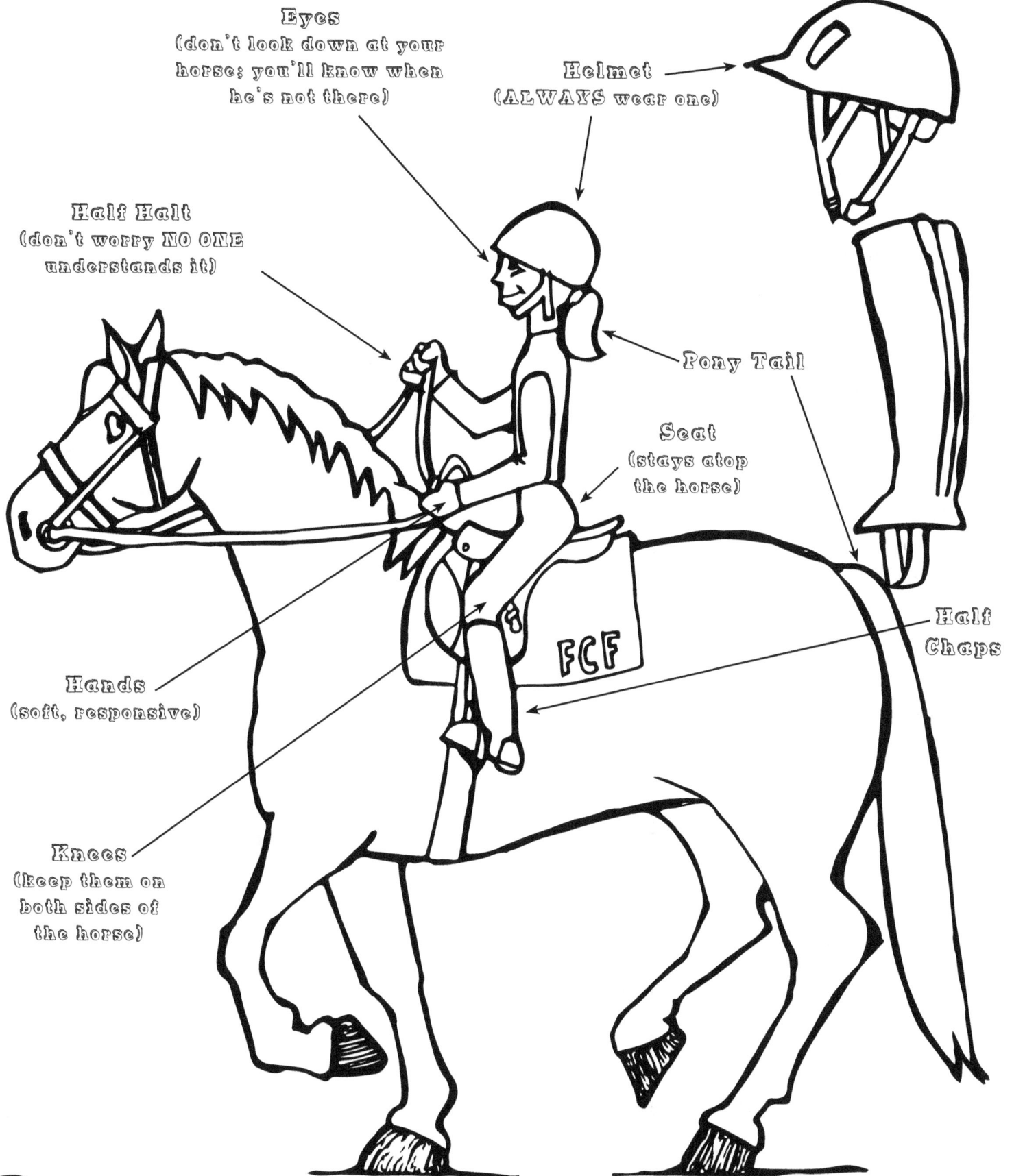

Eyes
(don't look down at your horse; you'll know when he's not there)

Helmet
(ALWAYS wear one)

Half Halt
(don't worry NO ONE understands it)

Pony Tail

Seat
(stays atop the horse)

Half Chaps

FCF

Hands
(soft, responsive)

Knees
(keep them on both sides of the horse)

Parts of a Horseback Rider

And You Must Know Your Horse

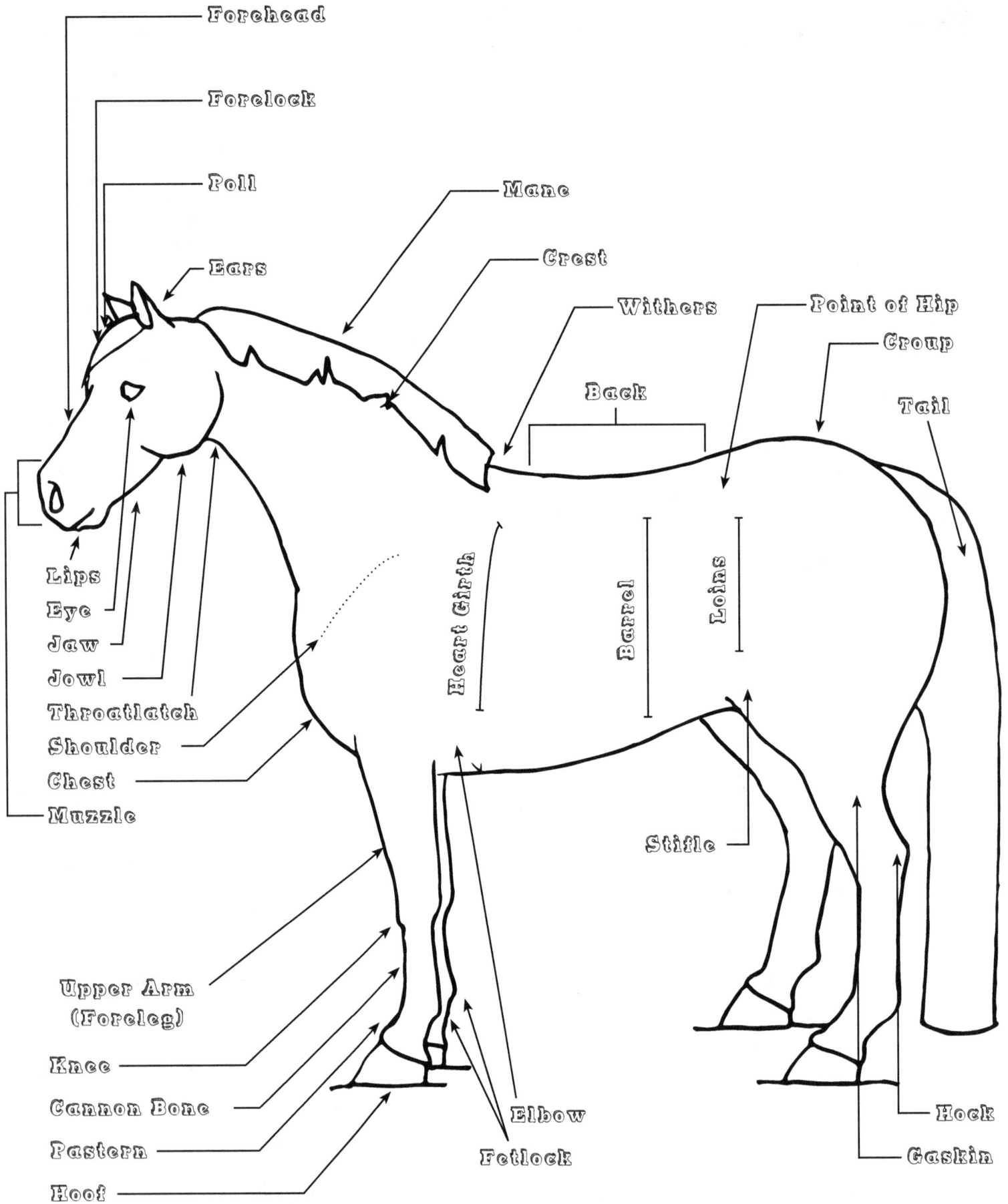

Forehead

Forelock

Poll

Ears

Mane

Crest

Withers

Point of Hip

Croup

Tail

Back

Lips

Eye

Jaw

Jowl

Throatlatch

Shoulder

Chest

Muzzle

Heart Girth

Barrel

Loins

Stifle

Upper Arm
(Foreleg)

Knee

Cannon Bone

Pastern

Hoof

Elbow

Fetlock

Hock

Gaskin

Parts of a Horse

Toe

Hoof Wall

White Line

Sole

Quarter

Bar

Center of Frog

Heel

Heal Bulb

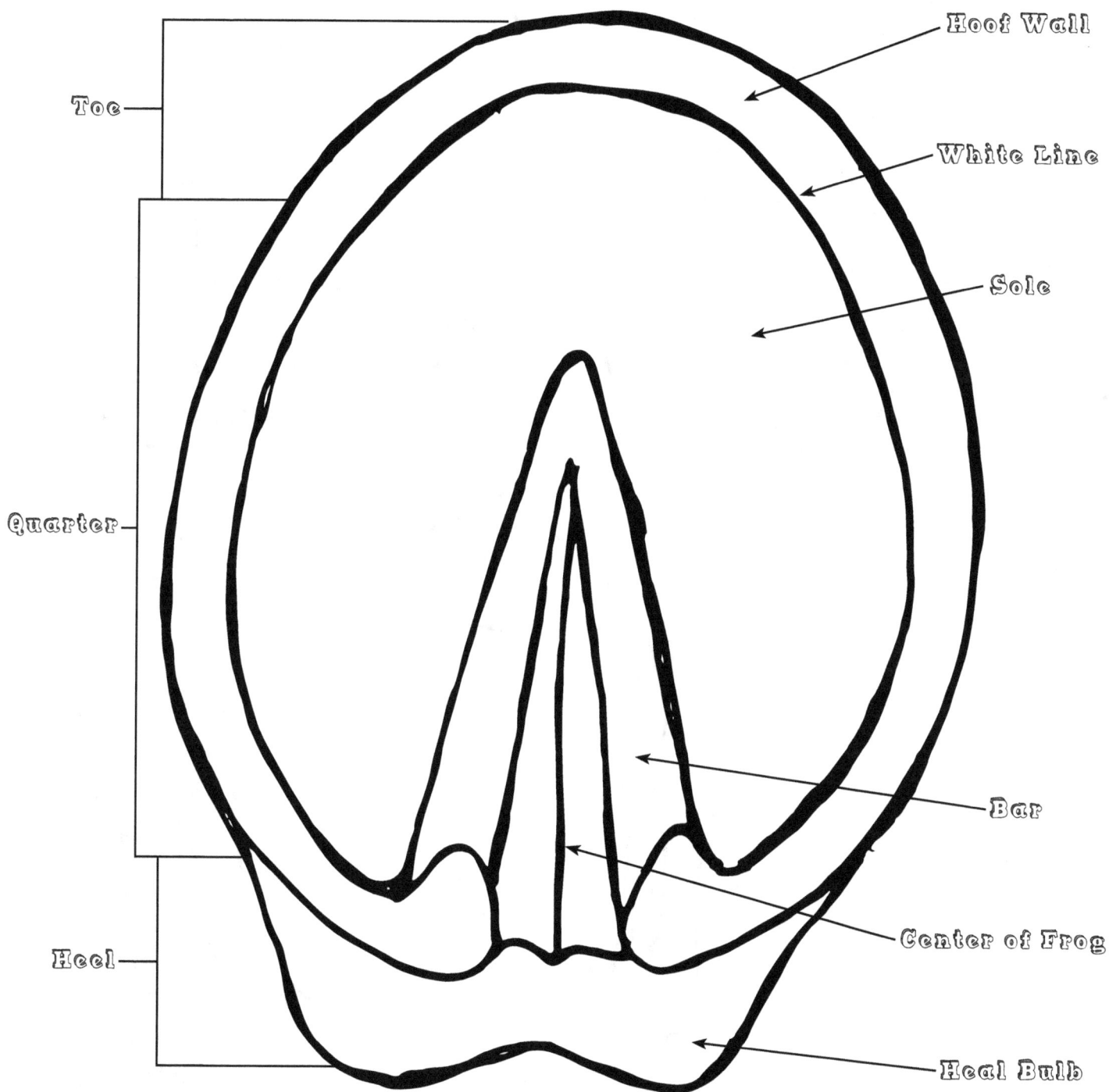

Parts of a Hoof

Star Fjord Mane

Stripe

Snip

Paint/Pinto Appaloosa Blanket

Chestnut

Ergot

Sock

Coronet

Stocking

Half Stocking Striped Hoof

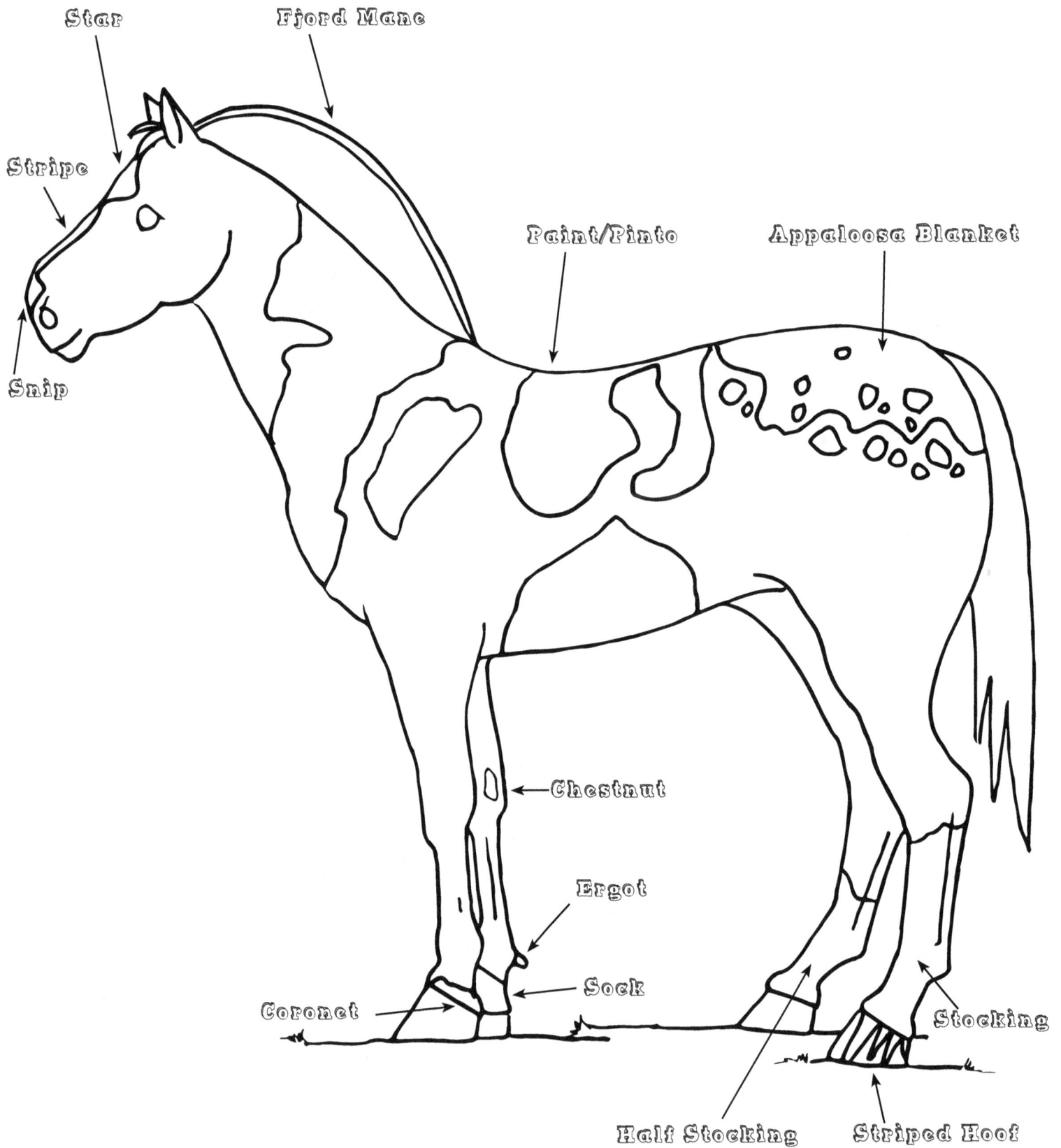

Horse Markings

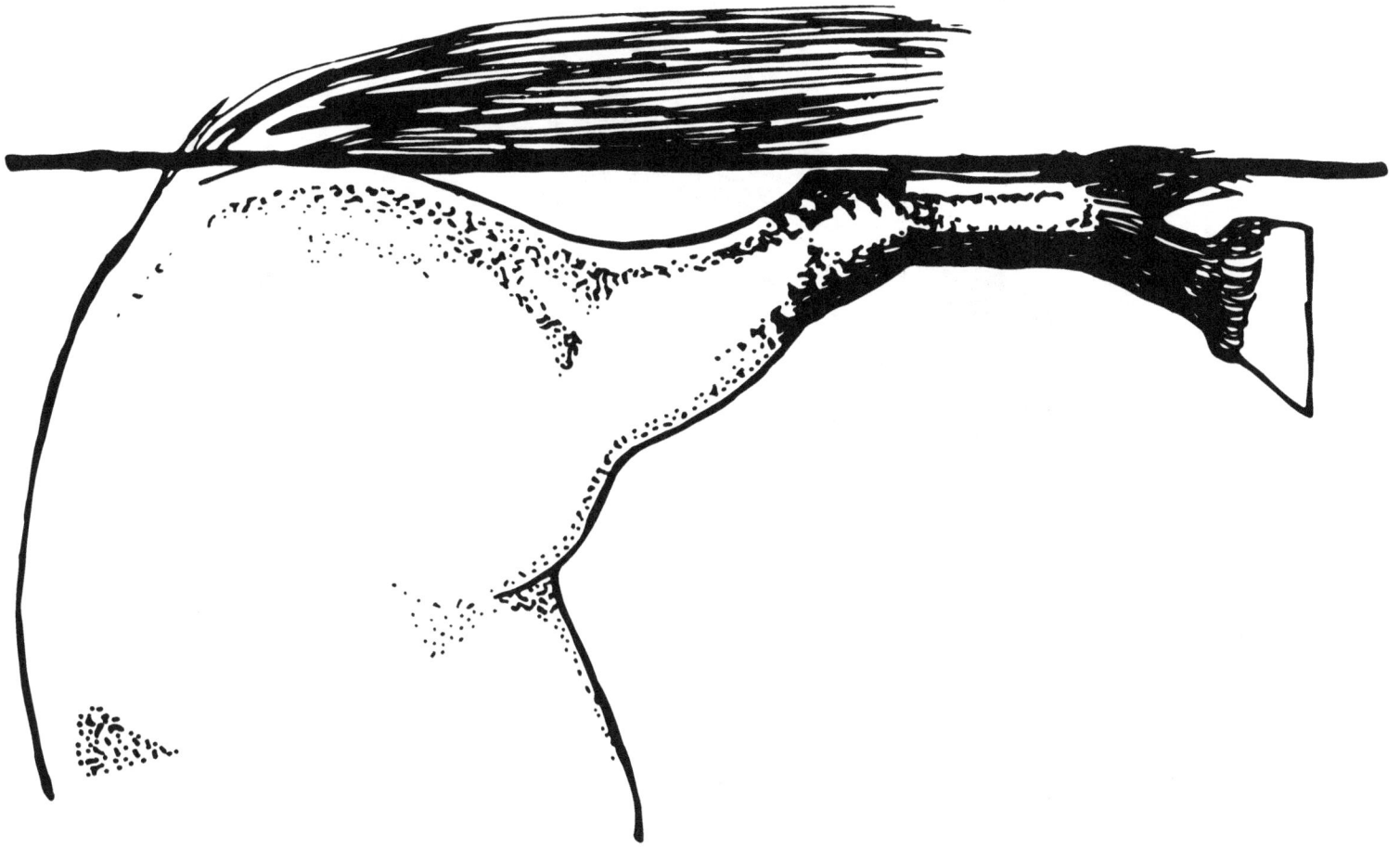

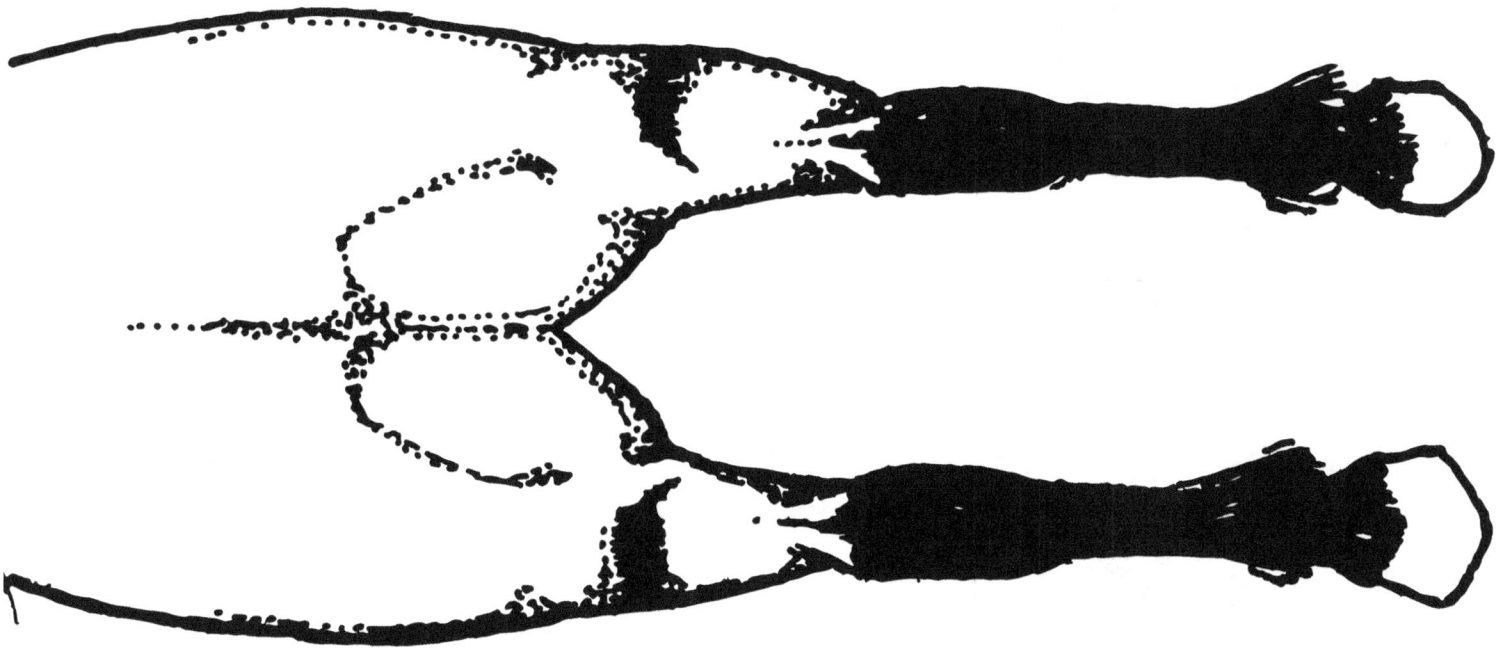

You'll Want to Know Good Conformation

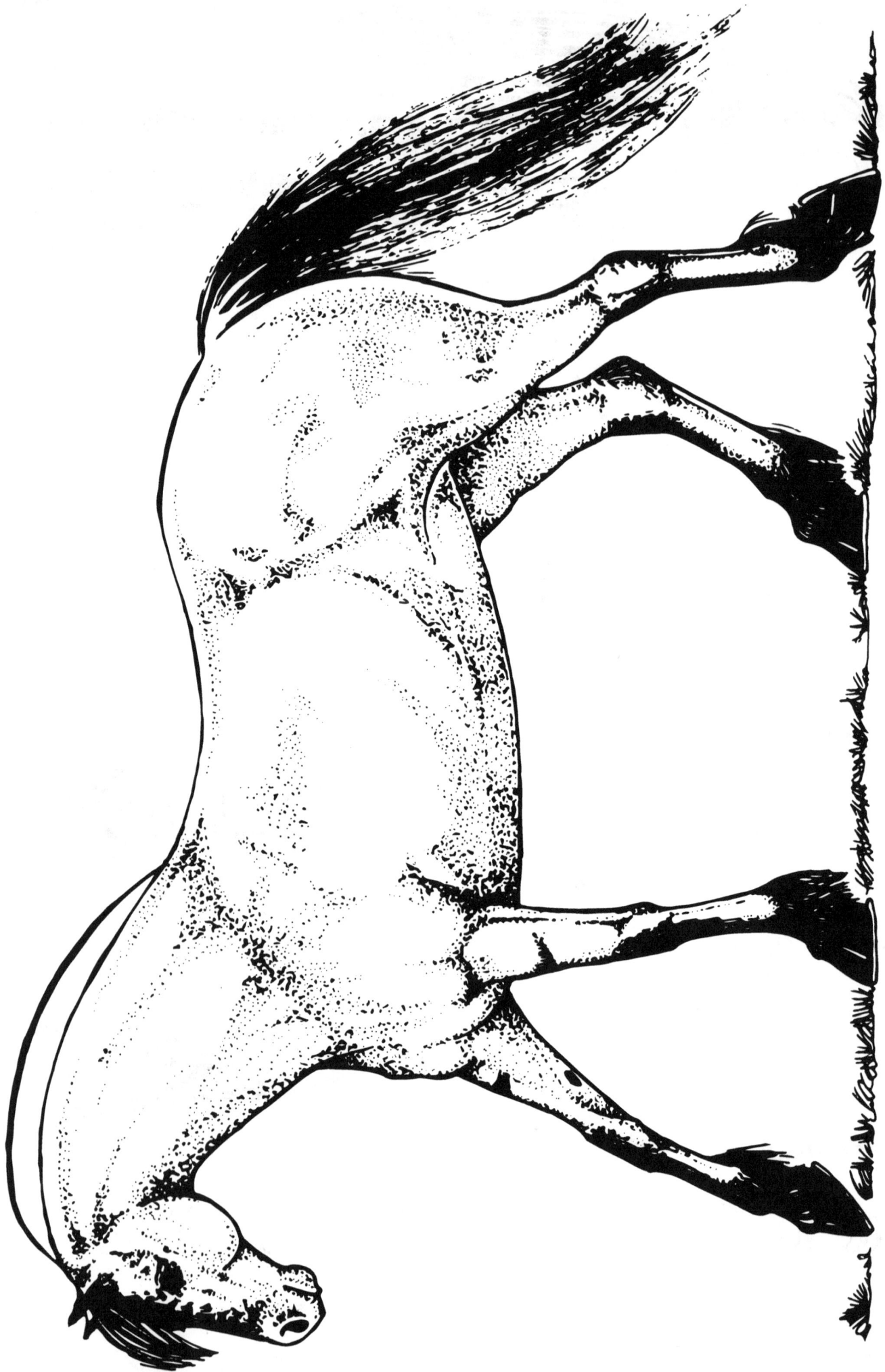

Collection is when a horse carries more weight on his hindlegs than his front legs. The horse draws the body in upon itself. Sometimes they need a little help.

FROM FRIENDS

Scores:
10 Excellent
9. Very Good
8. Good
7 Fairly good
6 Satisfactory
5 Insufficient
4 Fairly Bad
3 Bad
2. Very Bad
1 Not executed
-1 Should be executed

5   20
5 lbs
10 lbs
15 lbs
20 lbs
50 lbs

DQ

HALF PASS
PASSAGE
PIAFFE
TEMPI CHANGES
PIROUETTES

PRIX ST GEORGES
INTERMEDIARE I
INTERMEDIARE II
GRAND PRIX

MISSION IMPOSSIBLE LEVEL
TRYING AGAIN
BEGIN OVER
WHERE IS IT?
OH MY

Western and English horses move a little differently, because they have slight differences in their gaits. (Gallop and walk are the same.)

Jog

Trot

Western horses jog. English horses trot. Both are two-beat, diagonal gaits (the horse's right front and left rear hooves strike the ground at the same time). The only difference is the length of stride. The jog, while lively and ground-covering, is a shorter length, and therefore slower.

Jog vs. Trot

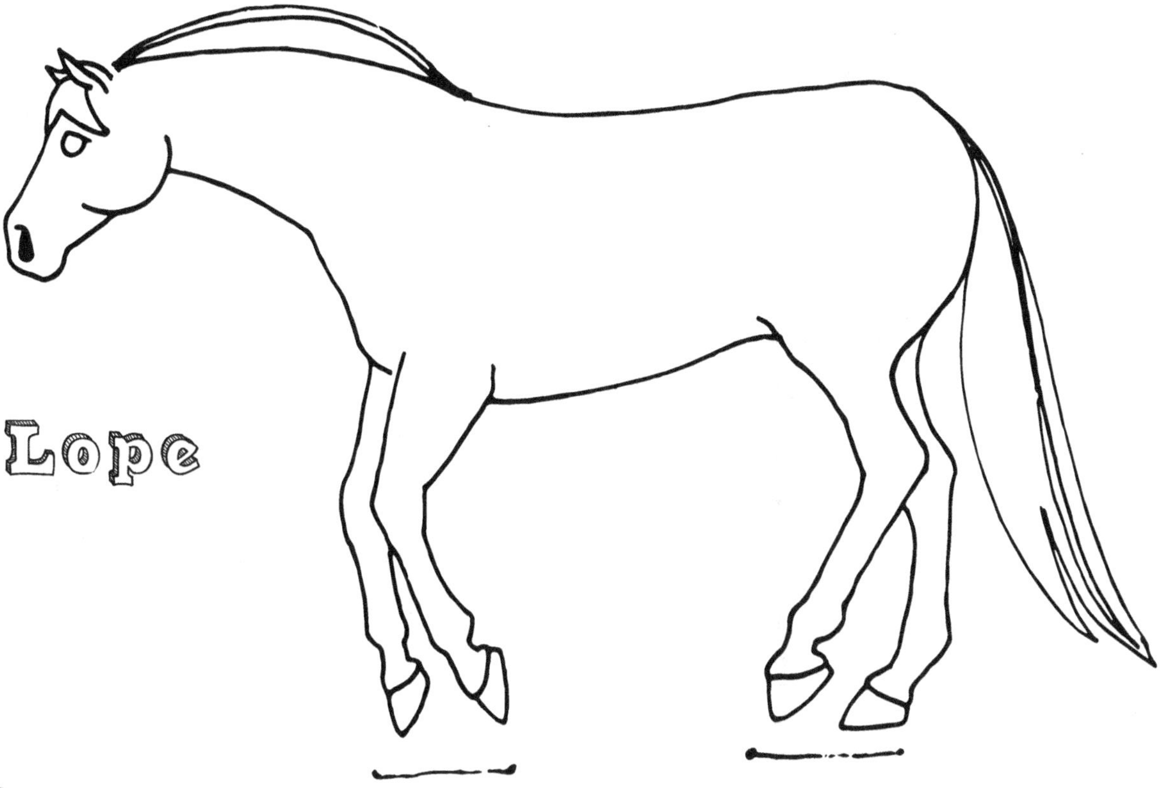

Lope

Canter

Western horses lope. English horses canter. Both are three-beat gaits. Like jog and trot, the only difference is the length of stride. The lope is a shorter length, and therefore slower.

Lope vs. Canter

Don't Forget About Grooming

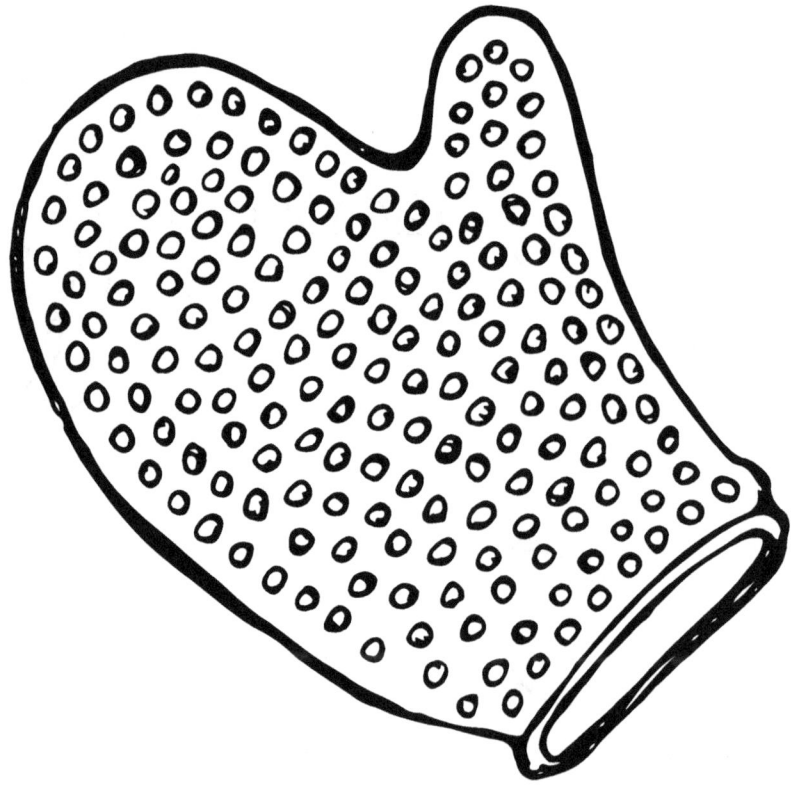

Hoof Pick

Mitt

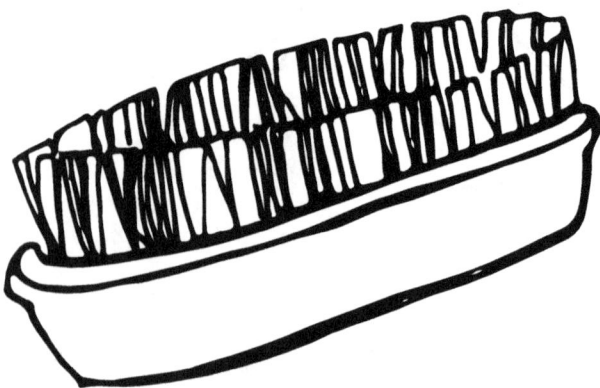

Brush

Curry Comb

Horse Grooming Tools

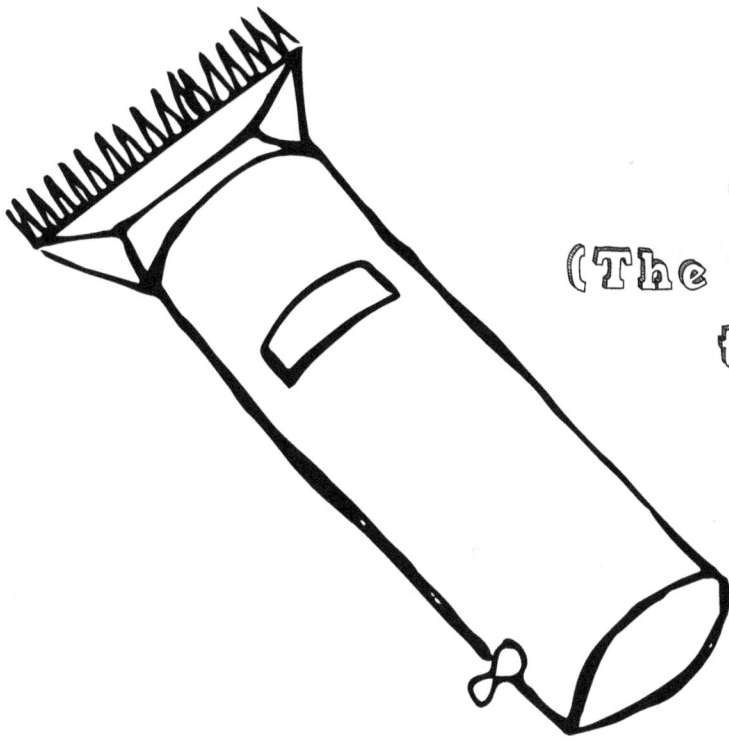

Clippers
(The MOST important
tool of ALL)

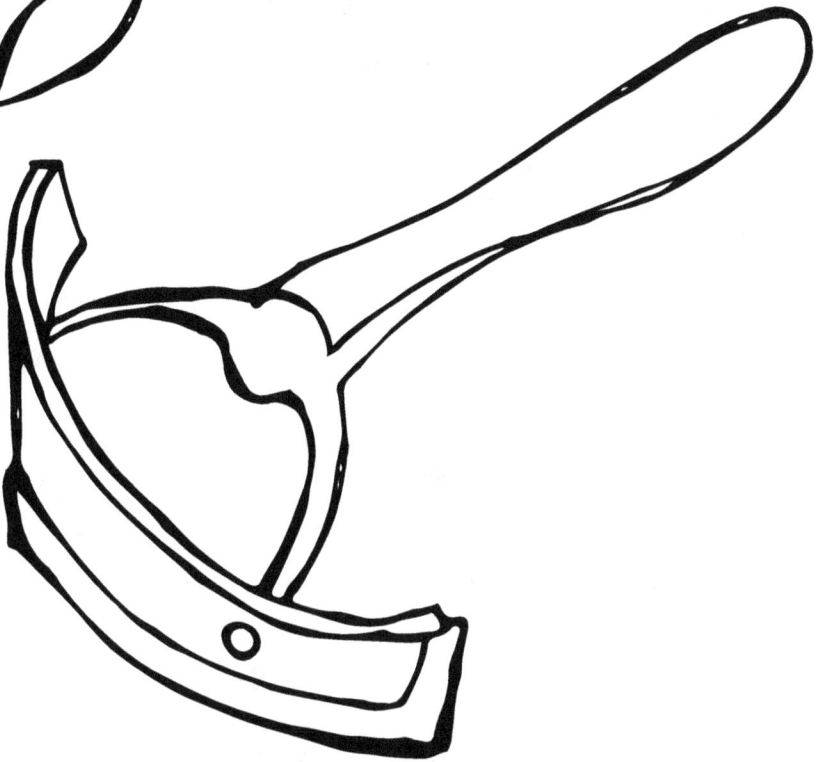

Squeegee
Scraper

Sweat
Scraper

More Horse Grooming Tools

There's an Awful Lot to Learn and
It Can Be Overwhelming

Learning Is Easier With
Proper Instruction

A good instructor will always believe in you, but you should still do your best to make her proud.

So You Want to Find a Good Instructor?

Aa Bb Cc Dd Ee Ff Gg Hh Ii Jj

DON'T RUN WITH CLIPPERS (STILL PLUGGED IN).

DON'T RUN THE JUDGE OVER AT "C"!

STAND

PICK UP FEET

No TROTTING IN HALLWAYS

DON'T BITE THE HAND THAT GROOMS you.

No PUSHING

No Kicking

C M B A H E K X

Some Instructors Are Strict ...

Some Instructors Are
Great With Horses ...

A Good Instructor Is Knowledgeable and Patient, and Will Teach You All Sorts of Things

Good Students Trust Their Instructor!

You'll still make mistakes.
And that's okay, because you
can learn from them, too.

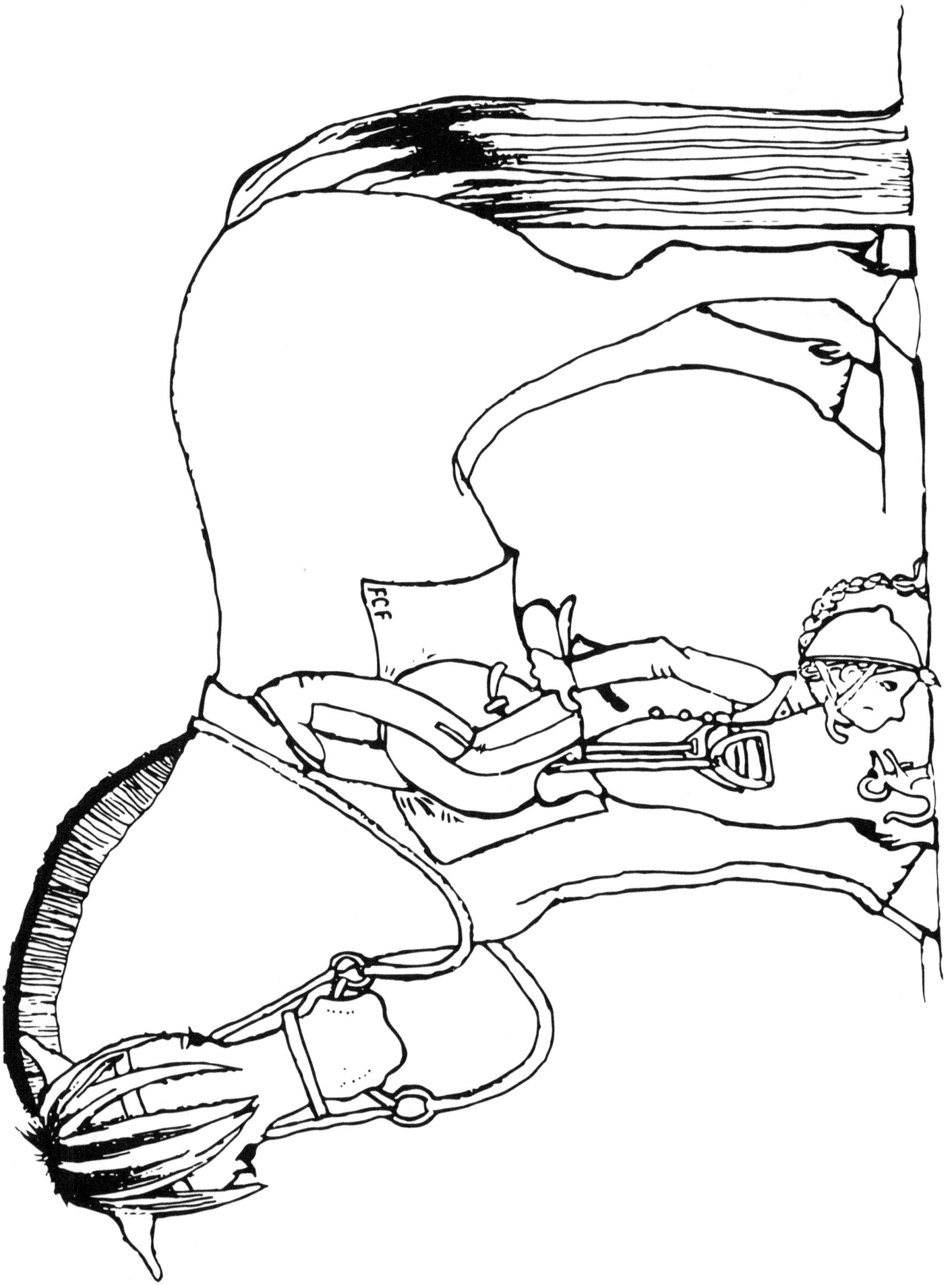

Even Horses Make Mistakes!

You'll Learn How to Handle a Horse

Safe, Effective Place to Lead

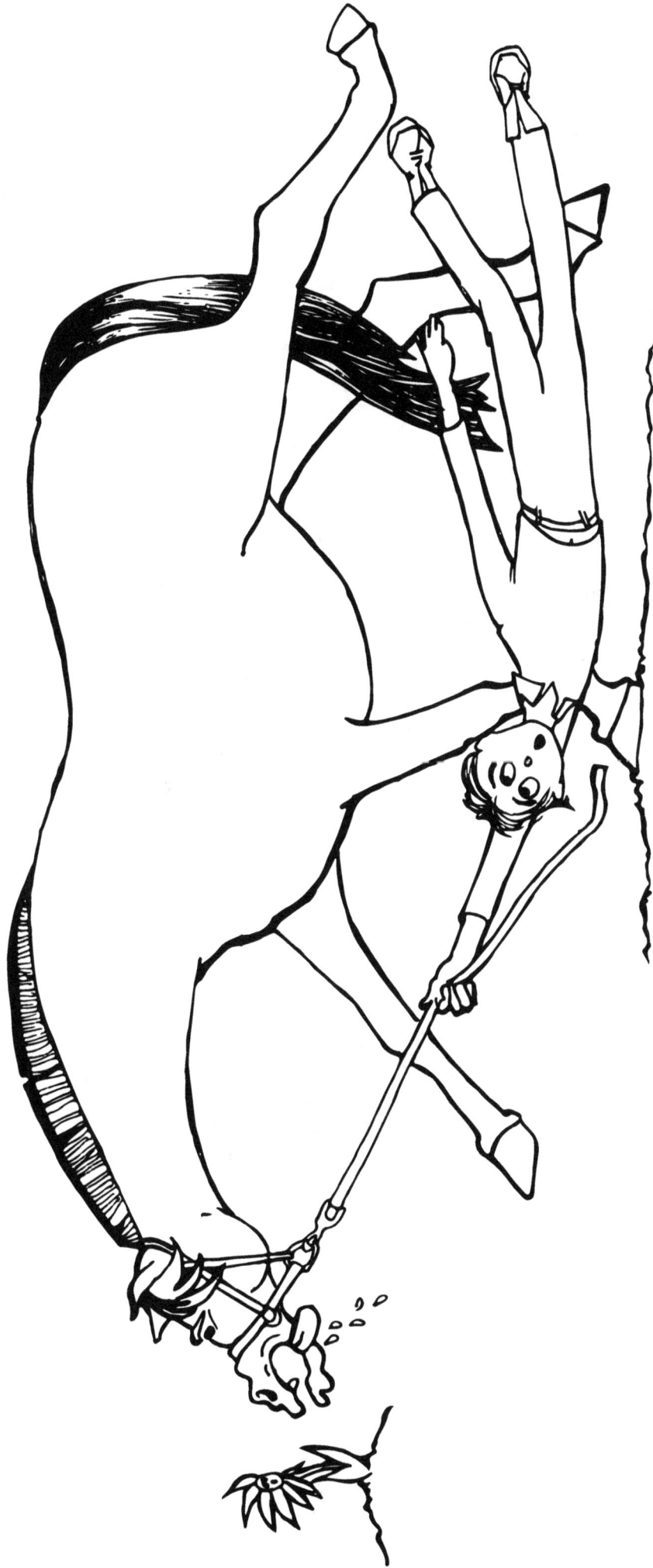

Less Effective Place to Lead ...

Correct Use of Cross-ties

Cross While Tied

Most Importantly; You'll Learn How to Ride

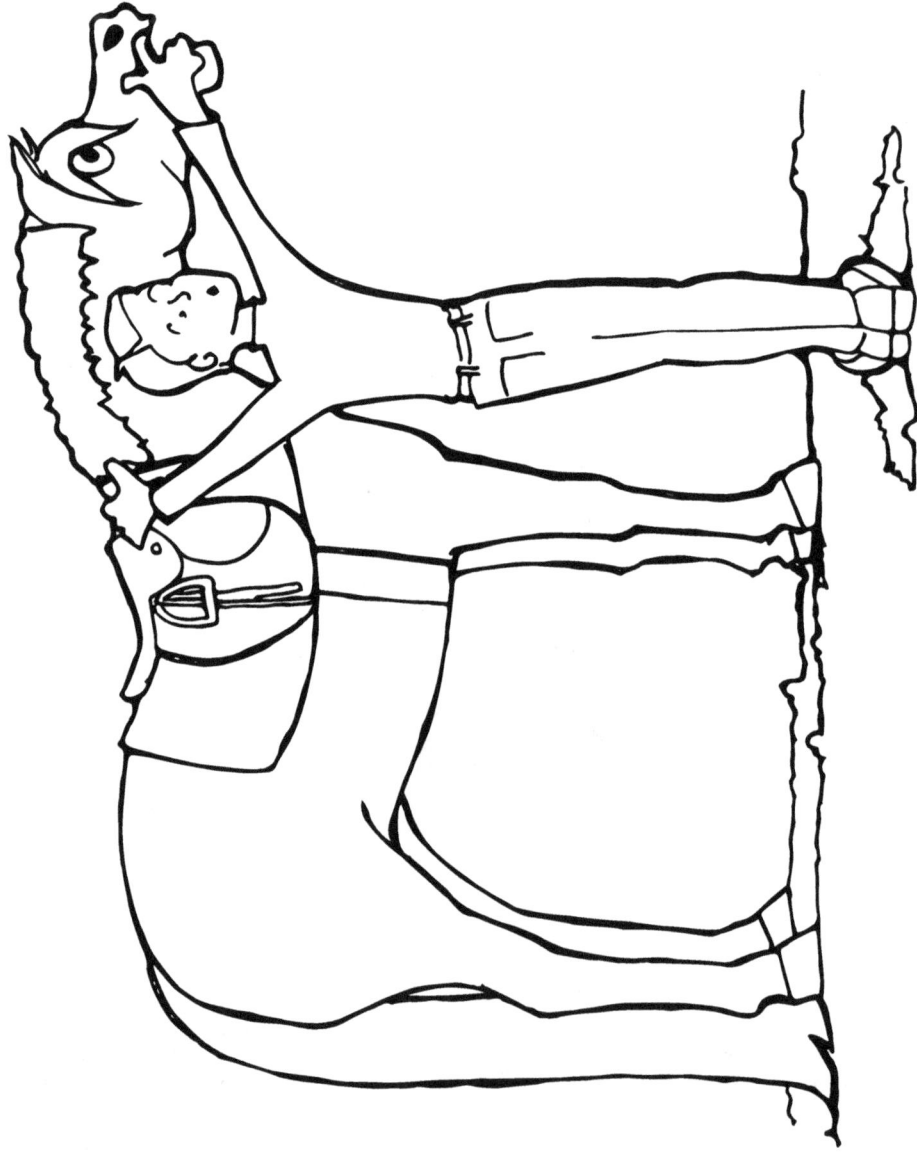

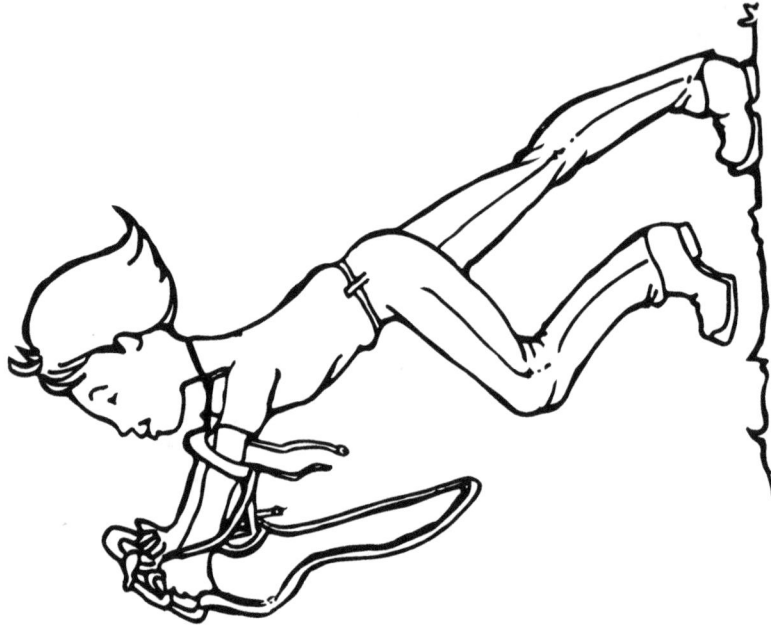

Introduce the Bit With Confidence

Can

C

Horses H   M Make

Edward's E   X   B Big

King K   F Fences

A

All

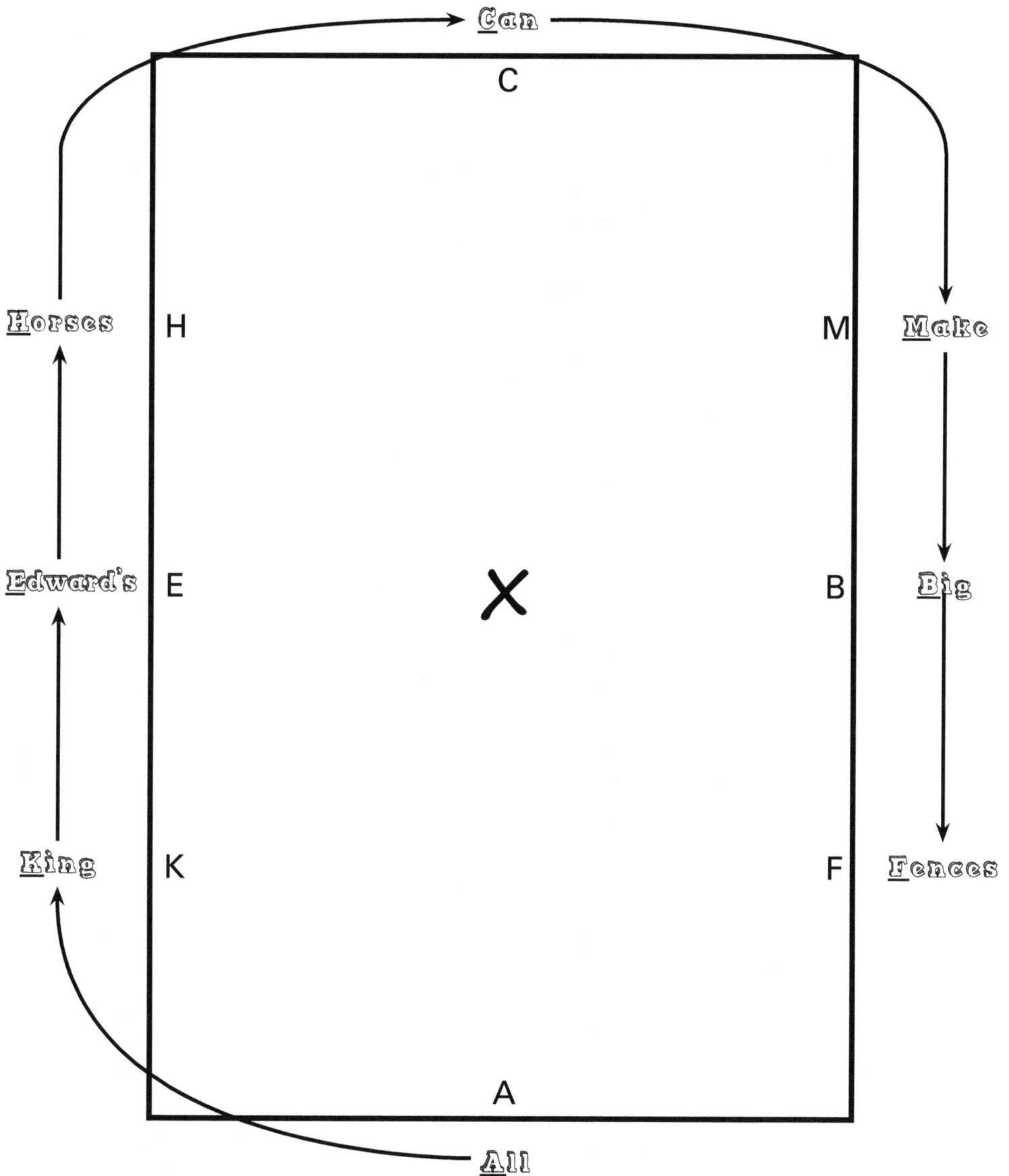

Dressage Arena
AKEHCMBF

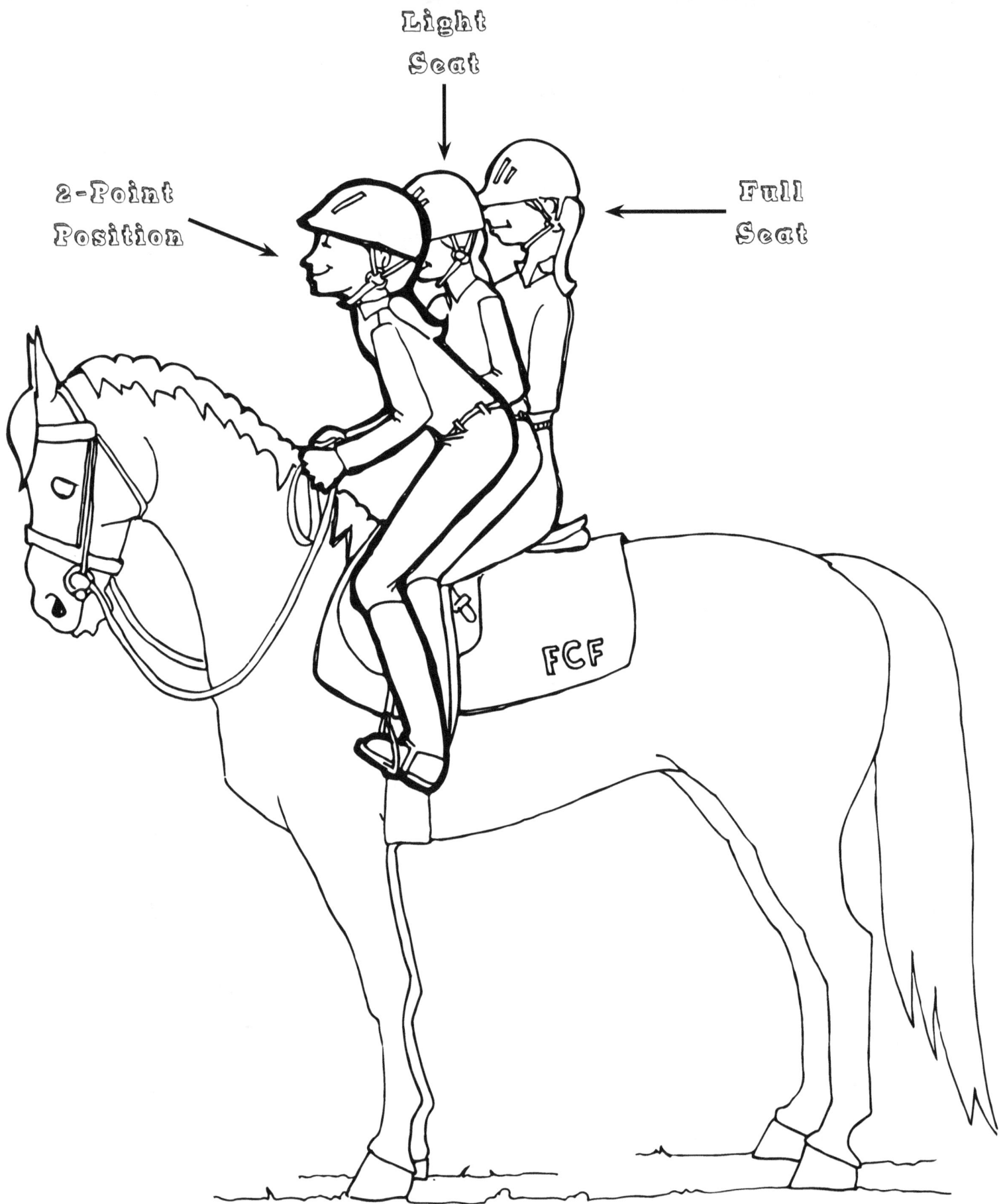

Light
Seat

2-Point
Position

Full
Seat

FCF

Seat Positions

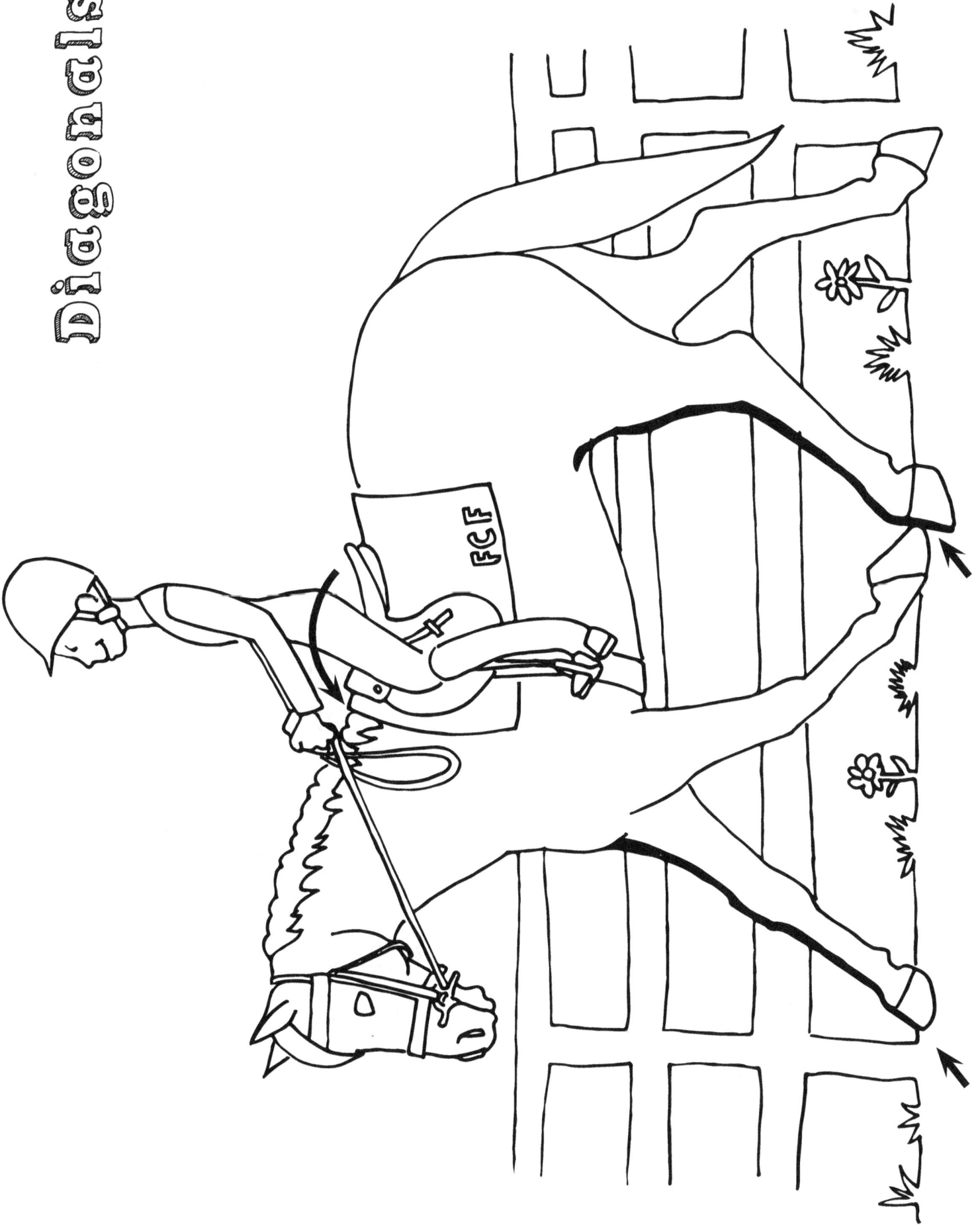

Diagonals

Keep a triangle behind the horse's shoulder

You'll Learn About Your Horse

Lunging is the perfect
way to OBSERVE your horse.
To SEE how your horse moves.
To SEE his abilities and weaknesses.
To take the edge off.
To teach voice commands.

Then you can decide what type of horse to buy/ride and what discipline to pursue

Horses come in all shapes and
sizes and colors and personalities.

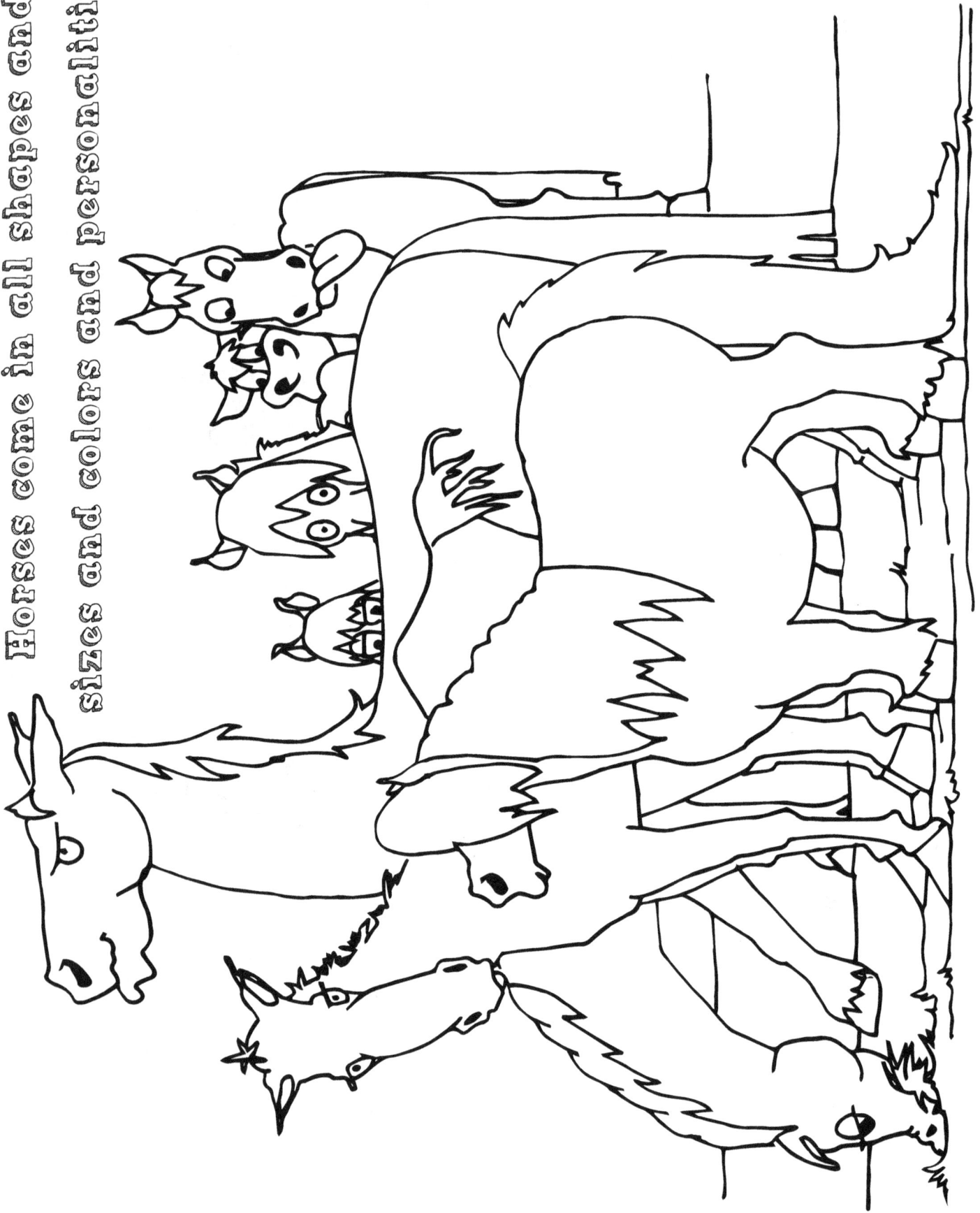

English Disciplines

Gaited Horses

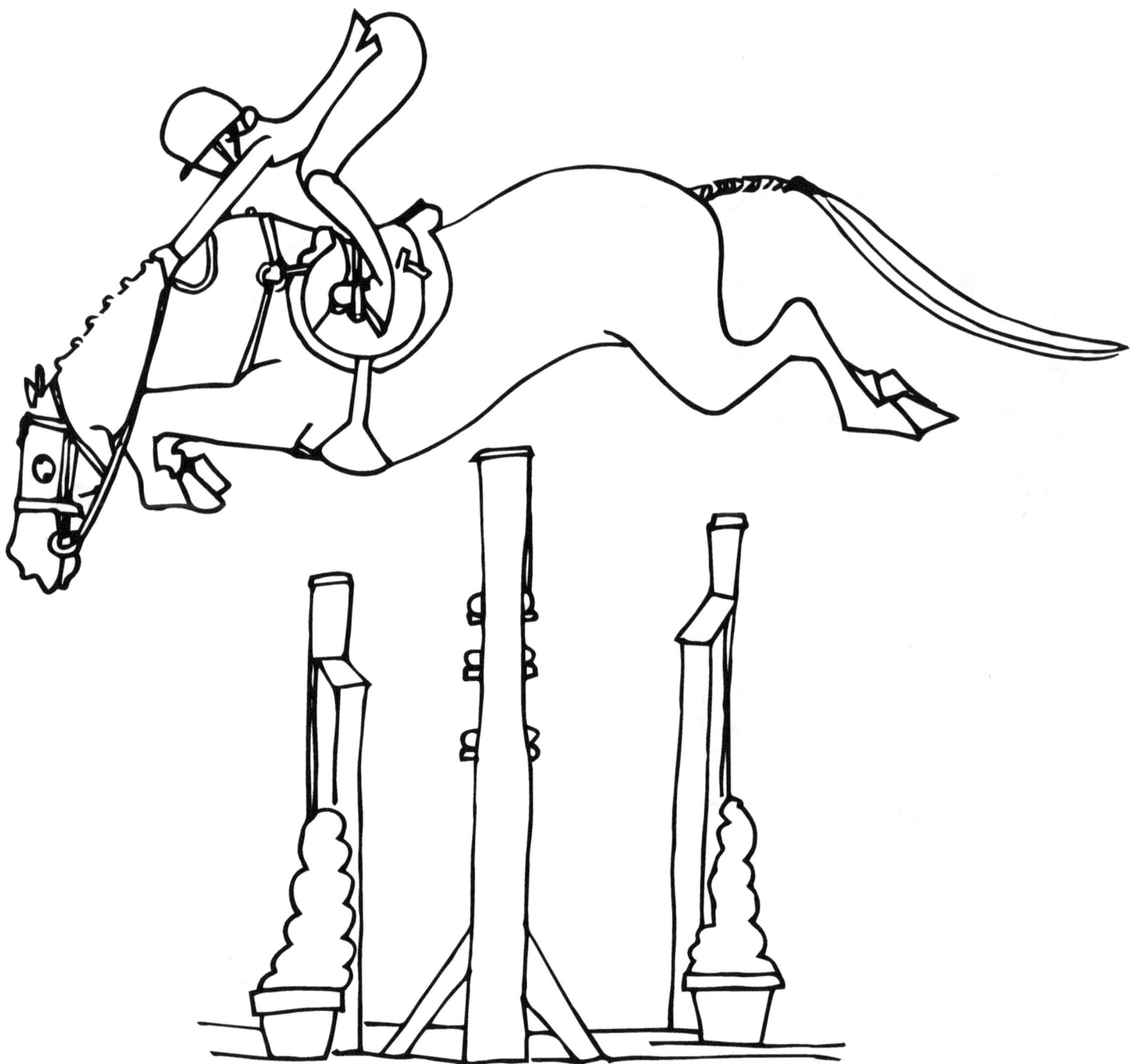

Jumping Horses

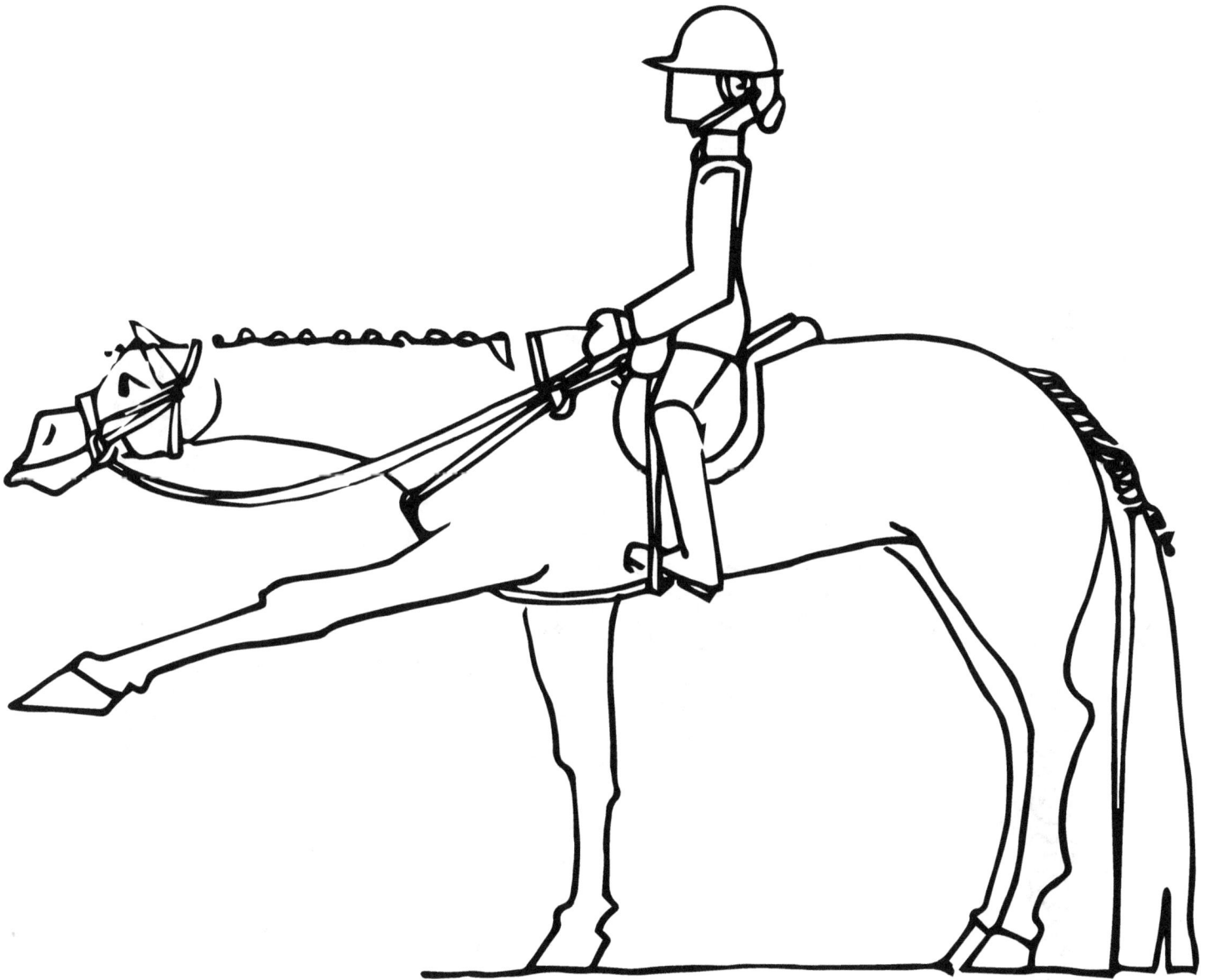

Hunter Horses

Western Pleasure Horses

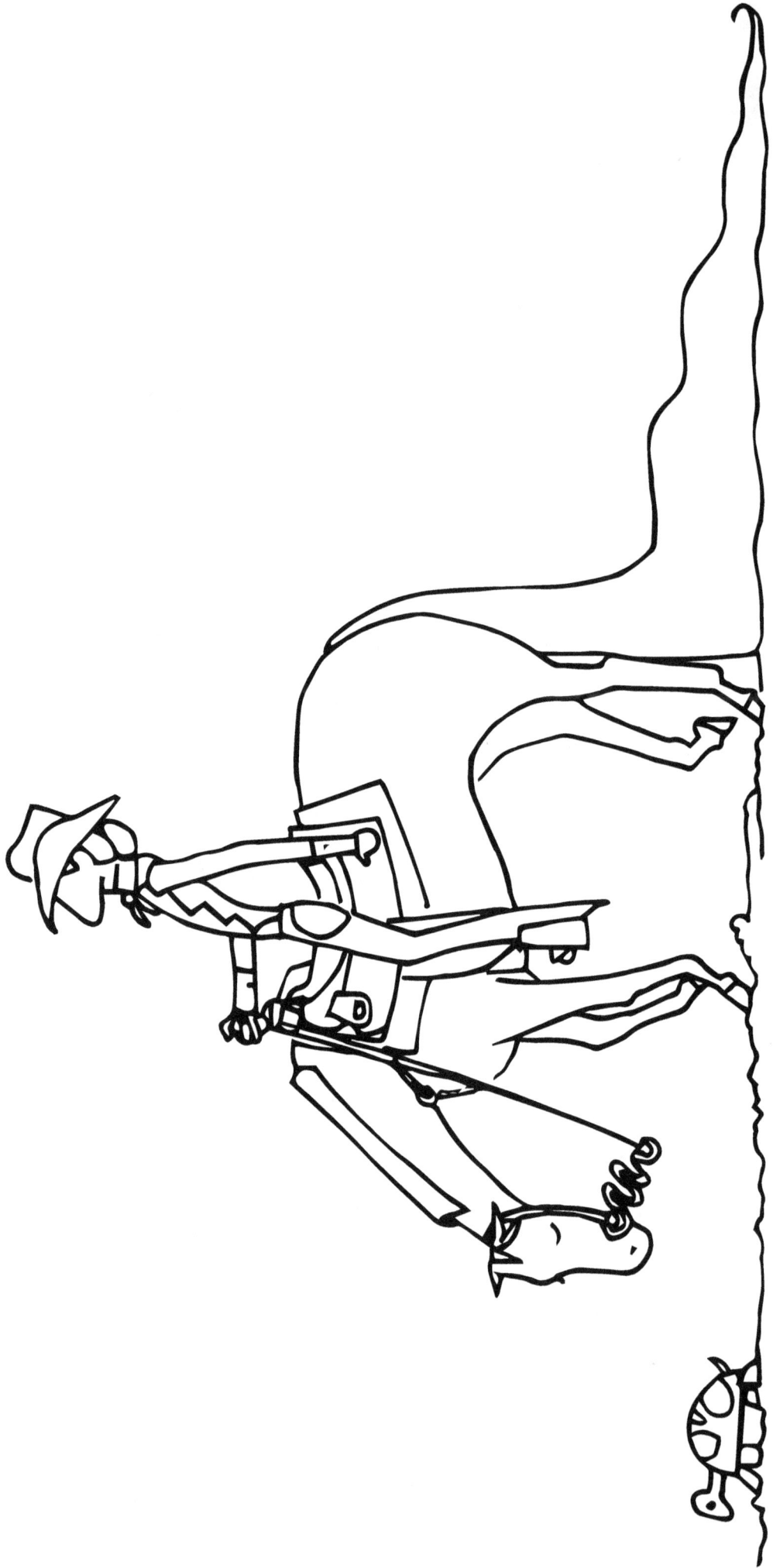

Dressage Horses

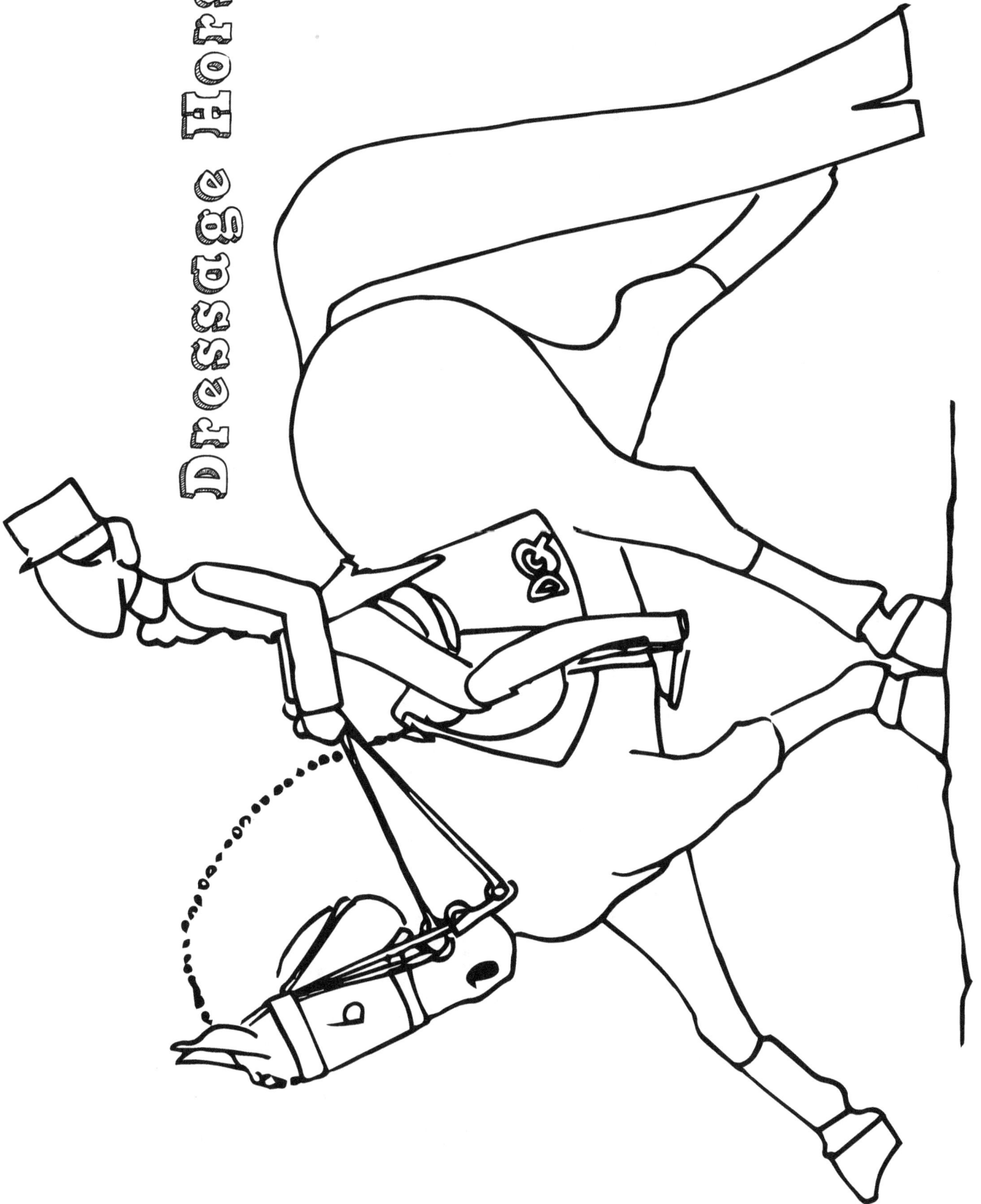

and Driving Horses

Western Riding isn't all roping cattle, baking beans, and settling in alongside a campfire!

Western

Disciplines

Barrel Racing

Reining (sliding stop)

Roping

Showmanship and Halter

Trail Riding

FINISH
1,250 MILES
(Really)

Endurance Rides

Western Pleasure

Western or English, some horses are a little shy.

and some are scared of everything on the trails, while others couldn't care less what they're passing. Western or English, we wish "Happy Trails" to you!

MEASURE YOUR LIFE IN LOVE

The Important Thing Is to Enjoy What You Do

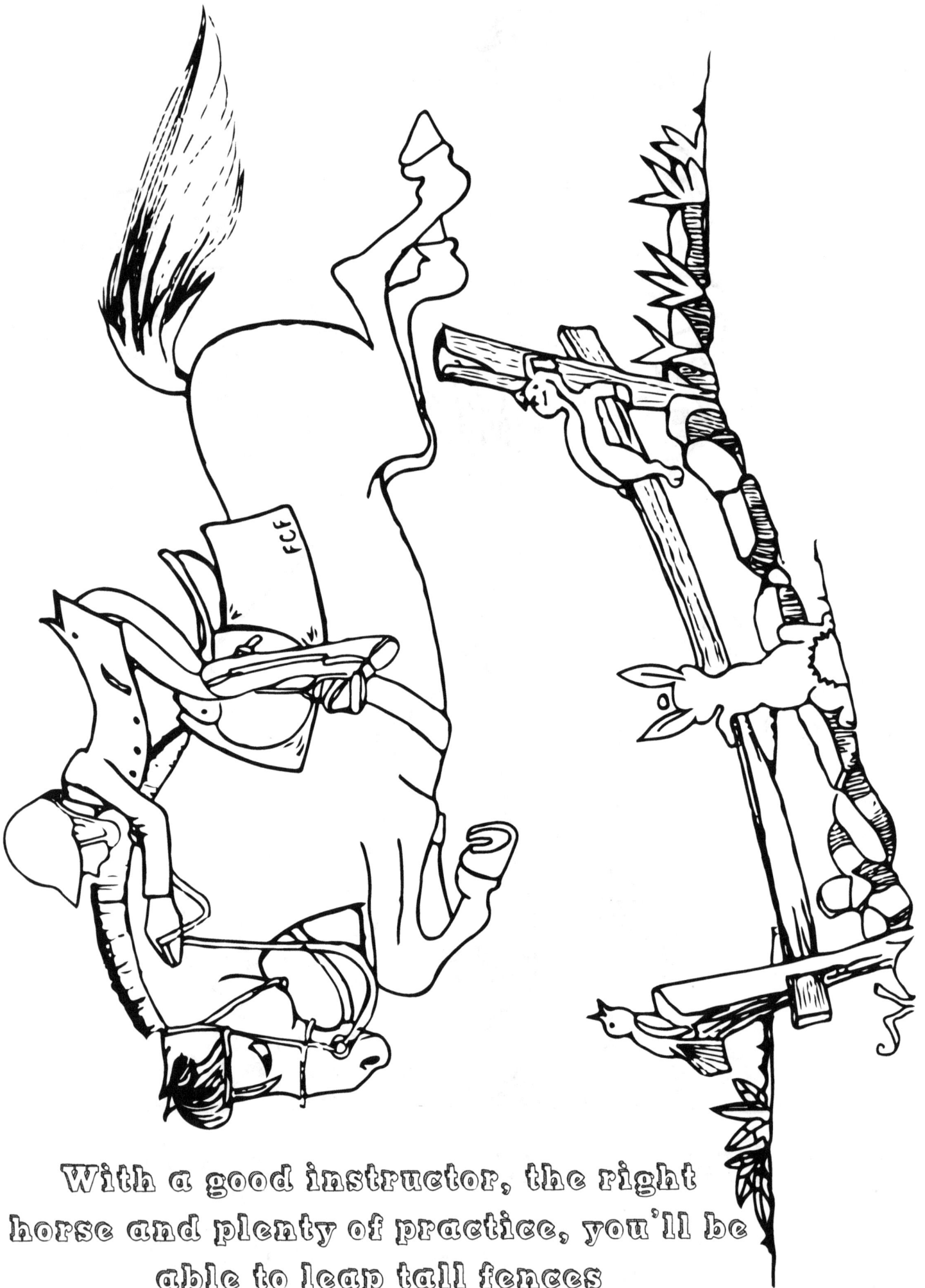

With a good instructor, the right horse and plenty of practice, you'll be able to leap tall fences

Fun Fjord Fact: Typically Fjord manes are well-kept with the black stripe 1/4" taller. When left to grow out they tend to look a little like a hippie!

Fun Fjord Fact: Many people believe all Fjords are fat. In reality, they're big-boned and big-muscled, but leave a Fjord in a lush pasture and it'll eat all day.

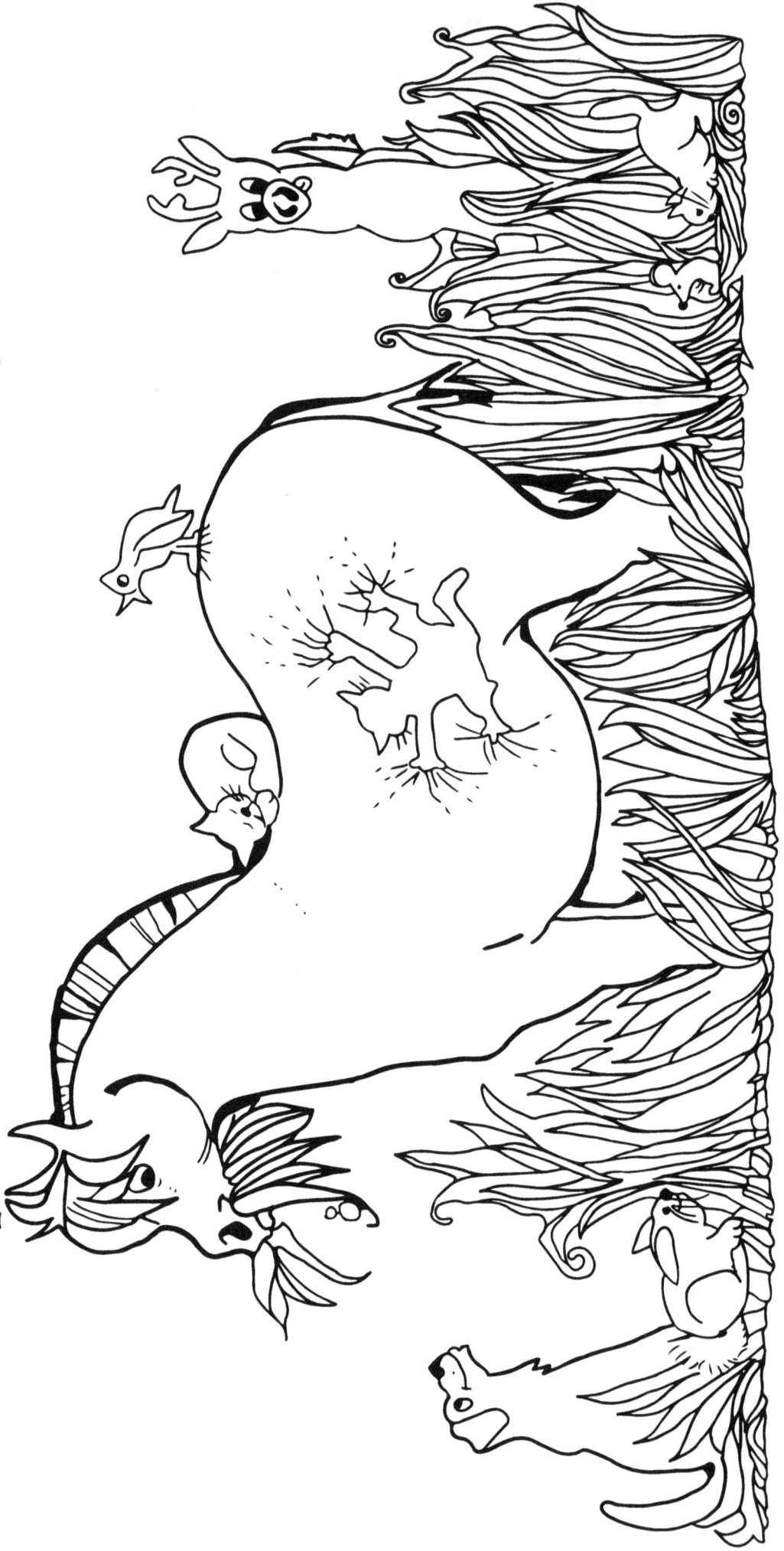

Fun Fjord Fact: People believe Fjord's tails and manes are spray-painted black. Nope. They're all natural.

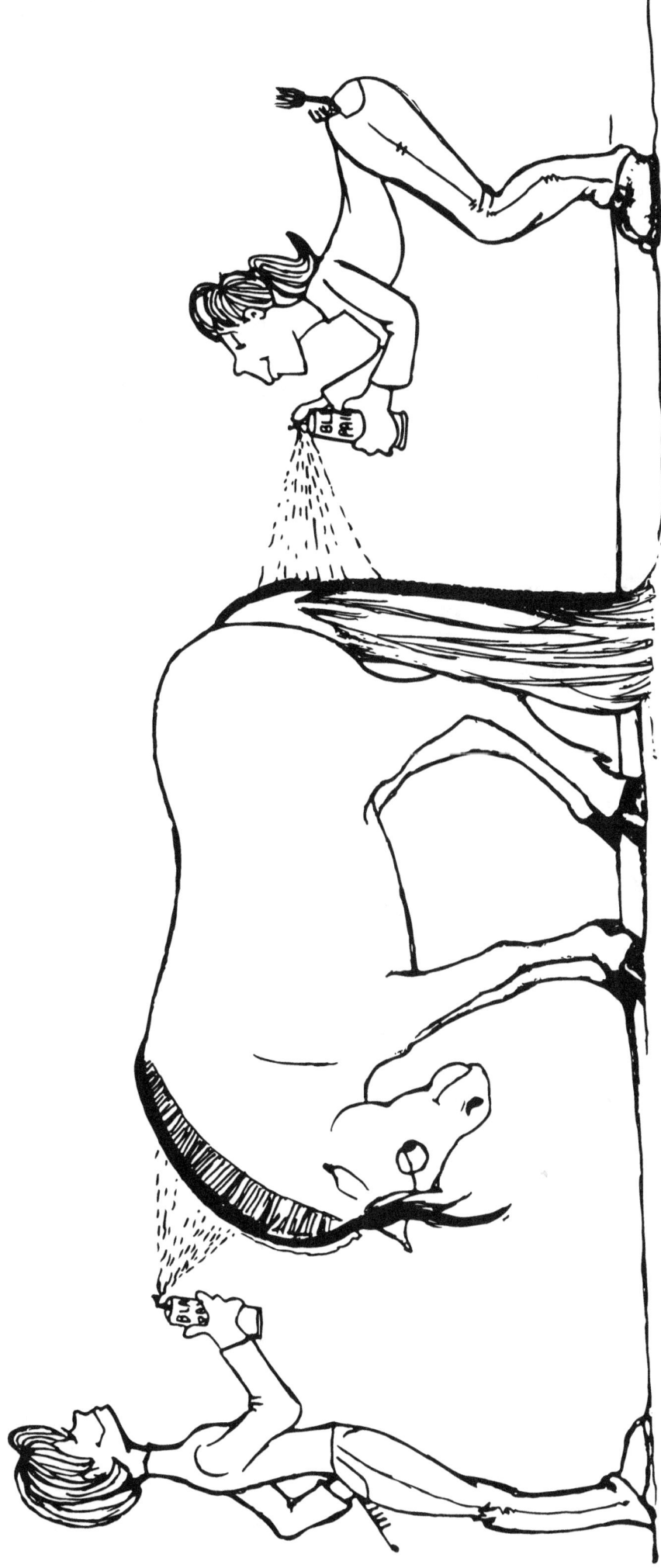

We're always working on new books!
Write to us (fcfwalter@gmail.com) with
your comments, ideas, or suggestions.

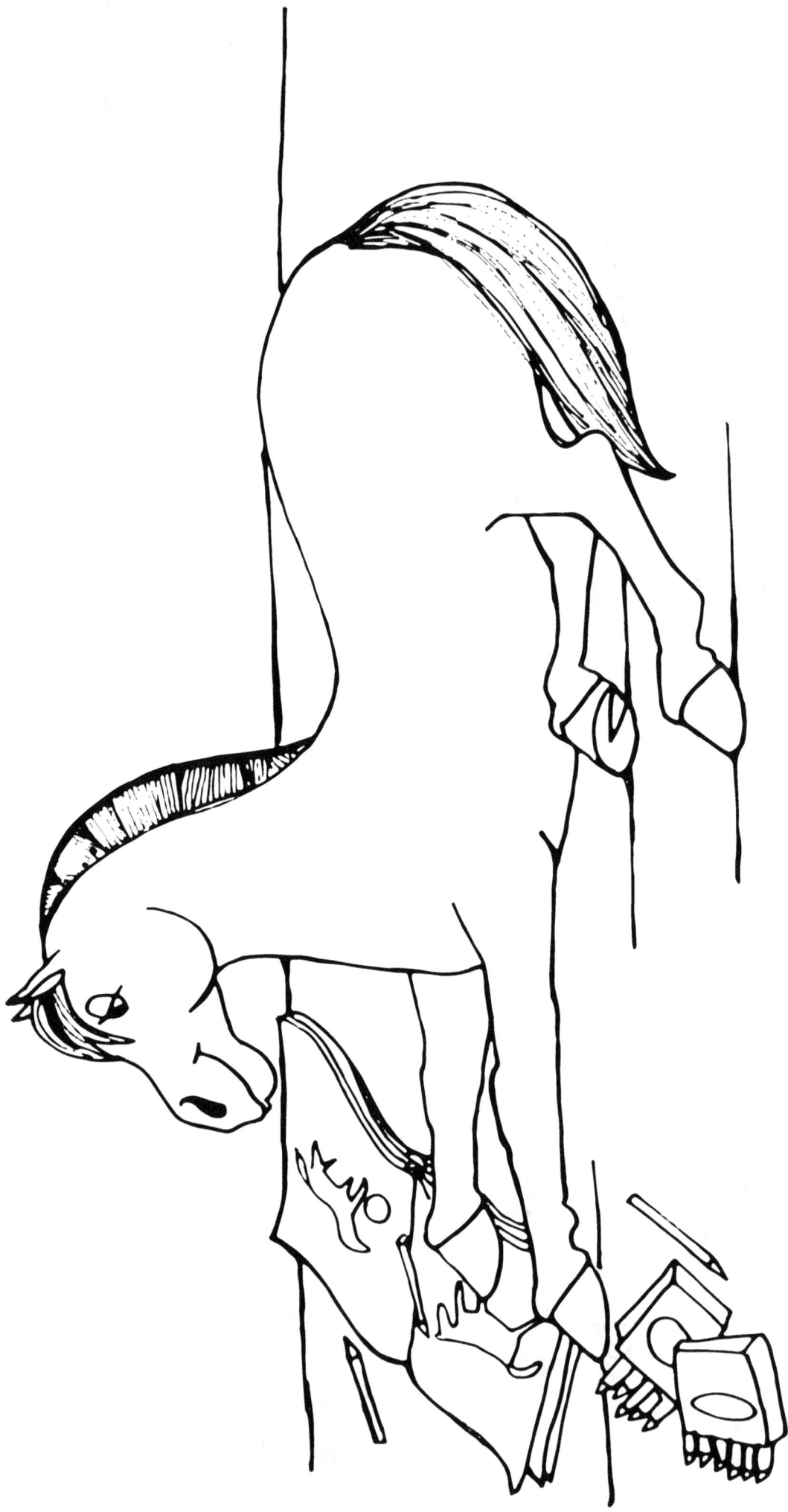

You might also like:

Color Your Way Into English Riding 1!

Color Your Way Into English Riding 2!

and ...
Color Your Way Into
A Horse for Christmas!

Francis Creek Fjords Coloring **Books**

Color Your Way Into
A Horse for Christmas

By Patti Jo Walter and Pat Holland